PSYCHOLOGICAL DISTRESS

SYMPTOMS, CAUSES AND COPING

PSYCHOLOGY OF EMOTIONS, MOTIVATIONS AND ACTIONS

Additional books in this series can be found on Nova's website
under the Series tab.

Additional E-books in this series can be found on Nova's website
under the E-books tab.

PSYCHOLOGY RESEARCH PROGRESS

Additional books in this series can be found on Nova's website
under the Series tab.

Additional E-books in this series can be found on Nova's website
under the E-books tab.

PSYCHOLOGY OF EMOTIONS, MOTIVATIONS AND ACTIONS

PSYCHOLOGICAL DISTRESS

SYMPTOMS, CAUSES AND COPING

HAYATE OHAYASHI

AND

SHUJI YAMADA

EDITORS

Nova Science Publishers, Inc.

New York

Library of Congress Cataloging-in-Publication Data

Psychological distress : symptoms, causes, and coping / Hayate Ohayashi, Shuji Yamada.
    p. cm.
Includes index.
ISBN 978-1-61942-646-7 (hardcover)
1. Emotions. 2. Distress (Psychology) I. Ohayashi, Hayate. II. Yamada, Shuji.
BF531.P79 2011
155.9--dc23
                        2011050990

Published by Nova Science Publishers, Inc. ✛ *New York*

CONTENTS

PREFACE

Psychological distress is a term used to describe the general psychopathology of an individual with a combination of depressive symptoms, anxiety and perceived stress. In this book, the authors have gathered and present topical research in the study of the symptoms, causes and coping mechanisms relating to psychological distress. Included in this compilation are topics corresponding to mitigating adverse school experiences and psychological distress with parental support; psychological distress in an oncological context; screening for psychological distress in clinical practice; the Kessler 10 (K10) psychological distress scale and psychological distress in the military.

Chapter 1 – Drawing on data provided by a nationally representative sample of adolescents studied at two points in time (N = 2,905), this study assesses whether perceived parental support can offset impact of adverse school experiences on adolescents' psychological distress, and if so, which parent's support, mothers' or fathers', is more effective. Analyses based on regression yield three noteworthy findings: First, Time 1 school experiences and fathers' support are each significantly related to Time 2 psychological distress after controlling for Time 1 psychological distress and other common correlates. Second, fathers' support significantly lowers the impact of adverse school experiences on subsequent psychological distress and this effect is similar for both boys and girls. Finally, for adolescent boys, mothers' support is inversely related to psychological distress only after adding the interactive term of negative school experiences and mothers' support to the model. These results are discussed in light of the theoretical literature and policy implications.

Chapter 2 - Psychological distress in oncology expresses the emotional suffering of patients due to cancer experience. Being diagnosed with cancer, from a psychological point of view means facing one's vulnerability and mortality. It also means experiencing exhausting and often painful therapies, and living with the possibility of relapsing or, in the case of progression, having to face new therapies. In all cases, a cancer diagnosis abruptly interrupts patients' life programs and dramatically upsets their daily routine. A percentage comprised between 22% and 45 % of cancer patients show moderate or severe distress levels, that impact negatively on the capacity to manage the disease, and on therapeutical adherence. In this chapter, authors will illustrate the psychological distress in an oncological context, providing a longitudinal perspective to evidence the different disease phases: from diagnosis to long-term survivorship or terminality. Authors will then attempt to determine the principal socio-demographic and clinical variables related to psychological distress. Being a "familiar disease", cancer affects the caregivers' well-being, too: in this chapter, the patterns of distress in oncological patients caregivers will be examined. Finally, the most common assessment tools for psychological distress used in oncology will be illustrated, along with some useful indications for its management.

Chapter 3 - Psychological distress is a term used to describe the general psychopathology of an individual - a combination of depressive symptoms, anxiety and perceived stress. The term poses a wider perspective to psychopathology compared to clinically diagnosed diseases, including also symptoms falling below the diagnostic threshold for a given disorder. Thus, especially in community and primary care settings screening tools for measuring also subthreshold psychological disorders and general psychological distress may aid early detection and timely intervention for people at risk. The 12-item General Health Questionnaire (GHQ-12), introduced by David Goldberg in 1972, is one of the most widely used and studied indicators of psychological distress. The prevalence of high psychological distress measured by the GHQ-12 varies from 15% to 36% across different studies, countries and by the cut-off points used. The GHQ-12 is associated with various sociodemographic and behavioural variables, which must be taken into account when screening for psychological distress in the population level. Screening for psychological distress in clinical practice is improved, when targeted carefully.

Chapter 4 - A large body of research has examined the relationship between work and physical and mental health outcomes, including psychological distress. While the main bulk of this research has addressed paid work, more recently unpaid domestic work (e.g. housework, childrearing) has also been considered. An understanding of the relationship between domestic work and psychological distress has been hindered by a lack of clarity concerning what consistitutes unpaid work, challenges and inconsistencies in measurement, along with a lack of guiding theory. This chapter considers these issues, reports on research conducted to date, and makes recommendations for future research examining unpaid work and psychological distress.

Chapter 5 - Among developed nations, Japan has one of the world's highest suicide rates. Mental health problems such as anxiety or depressive disorders are considered major public health issues, given that the likelihood of suicide is linked to these disorders. The aim of this study was to examine the prevalence of and factors related to psychological distress among employees in Japan. Employees from Akita prefecture in Japan were invited to complete self-administered questionnaires based on the Kessler 10 (K10) psychological distress scale. A value of 22 or higher on the K10 scale indicated high or very high levels of psychological distress. Furthermore, authors identified the relationships among the K10 psychological distress scale, socio-demographic status (sex, age, and education), employment-related variables (full-/part-time work, managerial class, job category, and working hours), and individual personality traits regarding internality-externality (locus of control scale). Analysis of data from 1,512 employees (males: 624; females: 888) indicated that the mean score and standard deviation of the K10 scores was 20.23 ± 8.04 (males: 19.52 ± 8.19; females: 20.74 ± 7.90), and that 37.2% of the employees (males: 33.7%; females: 39.6%) had high or very high levels of psychological distress (≥ 22 of the K10 scores). The mean scores and proportion of psychological distress on the K10 scale found in the present study were high as compared to those found in previous studies. The results of Pearson's χ^2 test based on the K10 scale regarding sex ($p < 0.05$), age ($p < 0.001$), education ($p < 0.05$), and job category ($p < 0.001$) showed significant differences between high or very high levels of psychological distress group (≥ 22 of the K10 scores), and the others. Furthermore, multiple regression analyses indicated significant effects in the K10 scale with respect to age, education, job category, and the locus of control scale. Data from this study can be used as K10 benchmark values to enhance the significance of future corporate health risk appraisal surveys. The results of this study may therefore help improve the understanding of psychological distress in employees.

Chapter 6 - Objective: Service members and their dependents represent a group who have been experiencing an increased amount of stress due to events such as multiple deployments and exposure to combat. As stress levels in the military rise and warfighters return from theater with complex psychological presentations, the need for evidence-based practices aimed at stress reduction becomes increasingly necessary. Mindfulness meditation is an evidence-based intervention that encourages individuals to bring their awareness to the present moment. Such practice can deliver the benefits of decreasing stress and pain and increasing emotional regulation. This manuscript explores the opinions of civilian and military providers working with the military population and their attitudes towards the utility of mindfulness-based practices for the military. The results from a two-day Mindfulness Workshop in Honolulu, Hawaii are highlighted. Insight into providers attitudes towards Mindfulness techniques may inform possible future applications for Mindfulness based interventions as well as future trainings. Methods: An anonymous self-survey titled Mindfulness Workshop Follow-up Questionnaire 1 (Post-Training) was administered to capture attending providers satisfaction with the Mindfulness training workshop. Results: 111 civilian and military providers responded to the questionnaire. Findings suggested that providers living in Hawaii were experiencing a high level of stress 7 (measured on Likert scale of 0-10 with 0 being no stress and 10 being extremely stressful). Attendees identified their superiors as being the group most in need of taking the Mindfulness training (79%). A large percentage of providers anticipated using this training in their personal lives (74%). Conclusions: Results of the survey confirm the body of literature cited that purposes a high level of stress present among the military population. Providers rated Mindfulness based trainings as being a promising tool to be used in a military setting as well as in their personal lives.

Chapter 7 - Infertile women in Japan as well as in the Western World have high levels of emotional distress, which include anxiety and depression. By cross-sectional questionnaire study, both scores of the hospital anxiety and depression scale (HADS) and the profile of mood states (POMS) for infertile Japanese women were high, indicating psychologically disturbed. In Japan, women are frequently greeted with traditional questions such as, 'Are you married? Do you have a child?' Elderly Japanese may project guilt on women without children, because they believe women should fulfill a role by producing an heir and/or heiress to continue the family name. This can cast shame and/or guilt on the infertility patients, and thus produce undo stress on women labeled as infertile. Therefore, infertile Japanese women should be supported by psychiatric intervention. In view of Immunology, natural-killer (NK) cell activity of the infertile Japanese women was significantly higher than that of the control. Elevated NK-cell activity is observed temporarily during stressful events. Persistent low NK-cell activity is associated with depression or stressful events caused by natural disasters. To the contrary, persistent high NK-cell activity is uncommon, however, increased NK-cell activity is observed in patients with recurrent pregnancy loss or Vietnam combat veterans diagnosed with long-term post-traumatic stress disorder (PTSD). A long-term chronic stress may underpin the basis for persistently high NK-cell activities. In consideration with high NK-cell activity for pregnancy, an embryo might be rejected from the uterus, because of its killing activity. Therefore, a randomized study was performed to clarify the effects of psychiatric group intervention on the emotions, NK-cell activity and pregnancy rate in infertile Japanese women. Thirty-seven women completed a 5-session intervention program and were compared with 37 controls. Psychological discomfort and NK-cell activity significantly decreased after the intervention, whereas no significant changes were observed in controls. The pregnancy rate in the intervention group was significantly higher than that of controls. Psychological group intervention was effective in infertile Japanese women. Finally, an interesting case was observed to achieve pregnant in a 50-year old Japanese woman with psychological relief. After failure of conception with 6 IVF attempts, the couple decided to discontinue further IVF treatment at age 48 years. One and one-half years later, she became pregnant naturally, resulting in getting healthy baby. During the time spanning her treatment for infertility, anxiety, depression, irritability, fatigue and grief were revealed to coexist with her high hopes of having a child. After termination of infertility treatments these adverse psychological findings were markedly lessened and her vigor was restored. Stopping infertility treatment might be a viable alternative for achieving pregnancy in similarly psychologically-challenged infertile women. Authors believe that reproductive psychology will be one of the main topics in the field of fertility and sterility in the 21st century.

Chapter 8 - Being diagnosed and treated for gynecologic cancer is an enormous physical and psychological challenge for the individual woman. During the course of treatment and even after, many patients deal with further life crises. In addition to the general stress caused by cancer, patients with gynecologic cancer can be vulnerable to distress associated with damage to self-image, altered sexual function, and loss of fertility. Authors conducted 3 studies on the theme of psychological distress among gynecologic cancer patients. The authors' results showed that patients experienced anger, fear, depression and anxiety, and authors recommend early psychosocial intervention for reduction of stressors, enhancing coping skills to manage stressors that cannot be reduced or removed, and establishment of a mental state and support system to maximize adaptation.

In: Psychological Distress ISBN: 978-1-61942-646-7
Editors: H. Ohayashi and S. Yamada © 2012 Nova Science Publishers, Inc.

Chapter 1

ADVERSE SCHOOL EXPERIENCES AND PSYCHOLOGICAL DISTRESS: THE MODERATING EFFECTS OF GENDER AND PERCEIVED PARENTAL SUPPORT

Ruth X. Liu[*1] *and Zeng-yin Chen*[2]
[1]San Diego State University, CA, US
[2]California State University, San Bernardino, CA, US

ABSTRACT

Drawing on data provided by a nationally representative sample of adolescents studied at two points in time ($N = 2,905$), this study assesses whether perceived parental support can offset impact of adverse school experiences on adolescents' psychological distress, and if so, which parent's support, mothers' or fathers', is more effective. Analyses based on regression yield three noteworthy findings: First, Time 1 school experiences and fathers' support are each significantly related to Time 2 psychological distress after controlling for Time 1 psychological distress and other common correlates. Second, fathers' support significantly lowers the impact of adverse school experiences on subsequent psychological distress and this effect is similar for both boys and girls. Finally, for adolescent boys, mothers' support is inversely related to

* Direct correspondence to Ruth X. Liu, Department of Sociology, San Diego State University, San Diego, CA 92182-4423, email address: rliu@mail.sdsu.edu

psychological distress only after adding the interactive term of negative school experiences and mothers' support to the model. These results are discussed in light of the theoretical literature and policy implications.

INTRODUCTION

Experiences at the school setting have an impact on many aspects of adolescent development, ranging from academic achievement to social-emotional well-being (Anderman, 2002; Eccles and Roeser, 2011; Roeser, Eccles, and Strobel, 1998; Wigfield et al., 2006). School, as an important context for development, may also give rise to stress which tends to have detrimental effect on adolescents' social and emotional adjustment (Compas et al., 2001; Eccles and Roeser, 2011; Flook and Fuligni, 2008). School-related stressful experiences for adolescents include exams, homework, relationships with teachers and fellow students etc. (Byrne, Davenport, and Mazanov, 2007; Suldo et al., 2009).

Like school, family remains a primary socialization context for adolescents. The importance of family factors such as parenting skills and parent-adolescent relationship has been noted by many studies. In general, effective parenting strategies and parent-child closeness tend to predict stronger academic motivation (Wentzel, 1998), fewer school-related difficulties (Repinski and Shonk, 2002; Shek, 2002), and more positive social and emotional adjustment among adolescents (e.g., Barrera and Li, 1996; Franke, 2000; Heaven, Newbury, and Mak, 2004; Shek, 2002).

Although family factors and school experiences are both recognized as separate contributors of adolescents' social and emotional well-being, few studies, however, have combined these two lines of research by asking whether family factors such as strong support on the part of parents can offset the impact of adverse school experiences on adolescents' psychological well-being. For example, does an involved parent matter when adolescents experience school-related difficulties? Can supportive parenting offset school-related stressors and their impact on adolescents' psychological outcome? These questions are important to address since concerns over the effect of parenting have persisted over the years. Some claim that parental factors may have been exaggerated (e.g., Harris, 1998). Others observe that school experiences may be more important to certain aspects of adolescents' adjustment than either the family or the peers (e.g., Crosnoe, Erickson, and Dornbusch, 2002; Elliott and Voss, 1974). Thus, by studying the extent of parental influence in offsetting school-related difficulties, we may not only gain a more accurate assessment of parental effect. More importantly, results from this research may yield practical implications as to how to build a better or more appropriate intervention program for adolescents at risk. Thus with this goal in mind, the present study extends the literature by assessing parental support in offsetting the impact of adverse school experiences on psychological distress among adolescents.

Studies on parent-child influence often question the relative importance of each parent. While some suggest that mothers' influence may be more important than fathers' (Quiery, 1998), others, however, insist that paternal involvement may be unique and thus is more important than maternal involvement (Flouri and Buchanan, 2003a; Harris, Furstenberg, and Marmer, 1998; Kernis, Brown, and Brody, 2000). Still others believe that the degree and importance of parental influence may depend upon gender of the child. Such claim is complicated by disagreements as to which parent-child linkage (i.e., same vs. opposite sex pair) may be stronger (Leinonen, Solantaus, and Punamaeki, 2003; Starrels, 1994; Videon, 2002). Furthermore, studies to date have seldom considered gender-specific effects of parental support in offsetting school-related adversities. This study thus examines which parent's support, mothers' or fathers', is more important in reducing the negative effect of school-related adversities on psychological distress among boys and girls respectively.

LITERATURE REVIEW AND HYPOTHESES

School Experiences and Psychological Distress

Adolescents' psychological health may be determined by a combination of factors known as stressors and moderators (of stress). According to Pearlin (1995), stressors are "problems, hardships or threats that challenge the adaptive capacities of people" (p. 3). Adverse school experiences may constitute a salient stressor for adolescents since negative experiences at the school setting may threaten to undermine adolescents' self-esteem. Self-esteem is theorized as an important protective resource for coping with stress (Greenberg et al., 1992; Taylor and Stanton, 2007). There has been consistent report that people with high self-esteem tend to be psychologically healthy whereas those with low self-esteem are more likely to feel distressed or depressed (DuBois and Flay, 2004; Orth et al., 2009; Taylor and Stanton,

2007). Interventions aimed at self-affirmation reportedly buffer psychological and physiological stress responses (Creswell et al., 2005). Symbolic interactionism views self-concept as based on the principle of "reflected appraisals", or the "looking-glass self" (Cooley, 1902; Mead, 1934), i.e., the individual sees him- or herself by taking the perspective of others. According to this view, individuals' self-concept is essentially based on how others view them. Adolescents with academic difficulties and troubled relationships with teachers and fellow students are likely to be seen as intellectually and socially incompetent. These adolescents may internalize the negative feedback received at school, which is likely to hurt their self-esteem (Cole et al., 1996). Studies have confirmed that perceived care from teachers predicts students' self-esteem (Eccles and Roeser, 2011). A dual failure model of depression argues that failures in the academic and social domains represent major negative life experiences for children, which are likely to result in psychological distress or depression (Cole et al., 1996; Patterson and Capaldi, 1990; Patterson and Stoolmiller, 1991).

Further, adverse school experiences may affect adolescents' psychological health by influencing their sense of belonging (Eccles and Roeser, 2011). A belonging hypothesis posits that humans have a natural need to form a minimum number of positive and lasting relationships. A threat to these bonds tends to result in negative affect (Baumeister and Leary, 1995). Feelings of belonging are posited to extend beyond interpersonal relationships to a broader sense of being connected to a larger community, and this sense of connectedness is found to predict both global and social loneliness. Indeed, feelings of being connected to a larger community such as school is another important factor, in addition to relationships with parents and friends, that has substantial influence on individuals' social emotional well-being (Chipuer, 2001; Pittman and Richmond, 2007). Studies have found that students' perceived relationship with teachers and a sense of classroom belonging are predictors of their education motivation and psychological adjustment (Burchinal et al., 2008; Eccles and Roeser, 2011, Roeser, Eccles, and Sameroff, 2000).

Parental Support as Social Resource

Contrary to the stressors experienced at school, supportive parenting from home may be an important social resource in moderating negative psychological outcomes. Pearlin states that moderators are "social and personal resources that can be mobilized to contain, regulate, or otherwise ameliorate the effects of stressors" (Pearlin, 1995, p. 3). Parental support which contains warmth and involvement on the part of parents may instill stronger self-control (Gottfredson and Hirschi, 1990), higher commitment to school expectations and success (Miliotis, Sesma, and Masten, 1999; Sui-Chu and Willms, 1996), and development of more effective social skills and coping strategies, which tend to be related to lower levels of psychological problems and poor adjustment (Heaven et al., 2004; Vazsonyi and Pickering, 2003; Whitbeck, Conger and Kao, 1993).

Further, supportive parenting may counteract the negative impact of school-related stressors. According to the "buffering" model (Pearlin, 1989, 1995), social support may protect, or "buffer," psychological well-being of the individual under stress through a number of mechanisms. With the presence of social support, the person under stress may redefine the situation as less threatening. Support may also assure the perceived coping ability. Finally, support may reduce the negative effect of stress by assisting problem solving, calming down the individual under stress, or promoting a positive coping behavior (Cohen and Wills, 1985).

As adolescents undergo adverse school experiences such as academic difficulties and problem relations with teachers and schoolmates, the most important coping resource to turn to is likely from parents. Family system theorists have long advocated that family is the first line of defense against threats to the psychological health of children and adolescents (Offer, Ostrov and Howard, 1981). The collapse of this protection is likely to make them more vulnerable against distress. Parental support not only helps adolescents' coping with stress, but also enhances their psychological adjustment (Vedder, Boekaerts, andSeegers, 2005; Way and Robinson, 2003; Wentzel and Watkins, 2002). Good parent-child relationships are reported to buffer adolescents' emotional well-being against stress (Wentzel and McNamara, 1999). Parental hostility, deficit in parenting skills (Ge et al., 1994; Ge et al., 1996) and parental rejection (MacPhee and Andrews, 2006; Magaro and Weisz, 2006) are associated with adolescents' depressive symptoms.

Supportive parenting may also indirectly buffer adolescents from adverse school experiences by protecting their self-esteem. Following the principle of "reflected appraisals" (Cooley, 1902; Mead, 1934), adverse school experiences are threats to adolescents' self-esteem due to the negative feedback of others from school. However, family constitutes another essential part of others for adolescents. Parental support may provide counterbalance to the threatening effect on adolescents' self-esteem from school. Empirical literature provides consistent evidence that perceptions of a lack of parental support and reports of parental affectionless control are associated with lower self-esteem (Mayhew and Lempers, 1998; Oliver and Paull, 1995). Warm and effective parenting provides a secure and positive home environment that boosts children's confidence and self-esteem, which is instrumental in fending off depression (Ge et al., 1994; Gecas and Schwalbe, 1986; Kenny and Barton, 2002; Kodak and Screery, 1988).

Studies of parenting over the years have used various measures for parenting practices. Regardless of the type of parenting measures used, the results are consistent across the board. The optimal or effective parenting practices, i.e., those that reflect the common core of warmth, involvement, communication, monitoring, etc., are consistently related to the positive outcomes of children and adolescents from academic motivation, behavioral patterns to psychological health (Amato and Fowler, 2002).

Maternal vs. Paternal Support

Although scholars generally accept that parents affect children differently, they tend to disagree, however, as to which parent-child effect may be more pronounced. In general, four arguments have been proposed concerning the degree of parent-child influence. The first argument recognizes greater importance of mothers' influence on children than fathers'. According to this contention, women tend to bear the primary responsibility of raising children. Hence, mother-child connection may be most critical to children's social and emotional development (Quiery, 1998). This contention has been supported by the observation that mothers tend to be the caregivers of the family. Furthermore, mothers often are the main socialization agents, such as by spending time with children and by being involved in school-related work with children (Larson and Richards, 1994; Montemayor, 1986).

Contrary to the above contention, others have noticed the unique influence of fathers in the family. Frequently, fathers are not only the main breadwinner; fathers serve as the family's main disciplinary figure. Furthermore, fathers who are involved tend to encourage children to be competitive and independent, and engage in physically stimulating interactions with children, which are beneficial to children's social and emotional development (Biller and Lopez Kimpton, 1997; Flouri and Buchanan, 2003b; Harris et al., 1998; Heaven et al., 2004; Kernis et al, 2000). Research has also confirmed that fathers' involvement and contact with children even after divorce are associated with children's academic success, positive psychological development and behavioral adjustments (Harris et al., 1998; Kernis et al, 2000). Reports also show that children's behavioral and emotional problems are connected with fathers' negative parenting (Shek, 2002) and characteristics (such as showing anger/anxiety) (Heaven et al., 2004).

Aside from the above two contentions, others have considered gender of children in addition to gender of parents (Leinonen et al., 2003; Starrels, 1994; Videon, 2002). Some proclaim the predominance of the same-sex parent-child influence such that fathers may be more important to sons whereas mothers are more important to daughters. This argument is based on the assumption that role similarities between parents and children increase the ties of the same-sex pair influence (e.g., Starrels, 1994). The opposite-sex argument, however, posits that the opposite sex parent tends to complement the same-sex parent in children's development. For example, fathers' encouragement of daughters in participating in feminine and masculine activities may promote daughters' sense of self and confidence (Sharpe, 1994) while mothers' relationship with sons may help sons' emotional and psychological development given women's general concerns over emotional connections with others (Dooley and Fedele, 2001).

Empirical studies by far have assessed the independent effects of parental factors on children's social and emotional outcomes. Findings from these studies generally support gender-specific parent-adolescent influence with some disagreements on the prominence of the same-sex vs. opposite-sex parent-child effects. This study, however, adds to the literature by exploring the extent of paternal and maternal support in counteracting the impact of adverse school experiences on psychological distress of sons and daughters respectively.

METHODS

Sample

Data are drawn from the National Longitudinal Study of Adolescent Health (Udry and Bearman, 1998). This longitudinal study is originally designed to investigate the health outcomes and well-being of youth in the United States. Using a school-based design, researchers select a stratified sample of 80 high schools with probability proportional to enrollment size and

52 feeder schools (junior high and middle schools) with probability proportional to the percentage of student contributions to the high schools.

Students in the selected schools respond to a self-administered op-scan questionnaire (known as the school data). Besides the school data, the researchers conduct in-home interviews with a core sample of students and some special over-samples (e.g., high education black over-sample). For the core sample, student rosters are obtained from each school and a random sample of 16,000 students is selected. Selected students participate in an hour and half in-home interview administered with the aid of a laptop computer. Sensitive data are collected with the audio computer-assisted, self-interview technology (Udry and Bearman, 1998). The present study utilizes the 50 percent of the in-home interviews contained in the public domain data (Wave I=6,504, administered from April-December, 1995 and Wave II=4,837, April – August, 1996).

Excluding high education black over-sample originally contained in the public domain data and using listwise deletion of the missing cases, the final sample includes 2,905 respondents, who participate in both Waves I and II interviews.

Variables

A total number of 12 variables (not counting interactive terms) are constructed. With the exception of the dependent variable, all of the variables are constructed from Wave I interview. For ease of interpretation as well as to avoid multi-collinearity problems, the variables are standardized (or put in the deviation scores) before entering into the regression models (see Aiken and West, 1991; Jaccard, Turrisi, and Wan, 1990 for details on methodology concern).

The dependent variable, T2 psychological distress, is derived from Wave II interview. They record seven additive items (α = .78 for boy and α = .83 for girl) of self-report experiences of feeling sad, depressed, lonely, fearful, and like a failure etc. during the week preceding the interviews. The responses range from '0' to '3', with '0' indicating 'never or rarely' to '3' indicating 'most or all of the time'.

The independent variable, adverse school experiences, is derived from Wave I interview (the same is for all other variables except for T2 psychological distress). It consists of 4 items that measure frequencies of experiencing school-related difficulties such as having trouble a) getting along with teachers, b) paying attention in school, c) accomplishing homework, and d) getting along with other students during the school year preceding the interview. The responses range from '0' for 'never' to '4' for 'every day.' Thus the additive index produces higher scores reflecting experience of more school-related difficulties ($\alpha = .67$ for boy and $\alpha = .70$ for girl).

The moderating variable, parental support is reflected in two measures of maternal and paternal support respectively. Maternal support is reflected in 9 items ($\alpha = .72$ for boy and $\alpha = .79$ for girl): 4 items include adolescent report of whether their mother has maintained involved by a) talking with them about personal problems, b) grades in school, c) things happen in school, and d) whether they and their mother have engaged in school projects together. The other 5 items measure degree of closeness adolescents feel with their mother, how warm their mother is, and how satisfied they are of the relationship respectively. Paternal support is measured by identical items to mothers with the exception that the reference is made about their fathers ($\alpha = .80$ for boy and $\alpha = .82$ for girl). Higher scores reflect stronger support from the respective parent.

Interactive Terms: To test whether parental support can offset adolescents from negative school experiences, two multiplicative terms are constructed by multiplying the standardized scores of adverse school experiences and support from the respective parent. Thus, the interactive terms are adverse school experiences x maternal support and adverse school experiences x paternal support. The interactive terms, however, are not standardized (Aiken and West, 1991).

A number of common correlates are constructed. They include T1 psychological distress, antisocial behavior, parental education, age, race or ethnicity, and family structure. T1 psychological distress is constructed with identical items as the dependent variable ($\alpha = .76$ for boy and $\alpha = .82$ for girl). Antisocial behavior consists of 15 items that measure frequencies of engaging in a series of illegal acts, such as stealing things, participating in group fights, drug dealings, and vandalizing other's property ($\alpha = .83$ for boy and $\alpha = .78$ for girl) during the past 12 months before the interview. The responses range from '0' to '3' with '0' indicating 'never,' to '3' for '5 or more times.' Parental education is measured by resident mother's education and missing values of mother's education are replaced with father's education if available. Four dummy variables (Black, Hispanic, Native, and Asian American) are constructed to represent race or ethnicity. Family structure indicates whether respondents are from intact family (intact = 1 vs. non intact =0).

Analysis

We test the hypotheses using regression modeling. The analyses are performed in stages. First, T2 psychological distress is regressed on adverse school experiences and maternal and paternal support with and without common correlates. These main effect models allow us to examine the independent influences of adverse school experiences and parental support on psychological distress over time. Following the main effect models, we estimate the interactive models with the interactive terms, adverse school experiences x maternal support and adverse school experiences x paternal support, added to the main effect models. If parental support offsets adverse school experiences as hypothesized, we shall observe interactive terms to be inversely related to the dependent variable. In other words, support from the respective parent reduces the adverse effect of school experiences on psychological distress. All of these models are estimated both among the total group and by gender. Furthermore, throughout the analysis, regression coefficients are weighted using sampling weights (derived from Wave II interview) and significance tests are conducted using robust standard errors obtained by adjusting for the clustering effects.

RESULTS

Before estimating regression models, we obtain descriptive statistics of the variables used in the analyses. Thus, means or proportions and standard deviations of the variables for the total group and by gender are shown in Table 1.

As seen (in Table 1), boys on average report slightly lower levels of psychological distress, higher levels of negative school experiences and parental support, and higher levels of antisocial behavior than girls. Other than these variables of interest, boys and girls are quite similar, especially in regard to parental education, family structure, and race/ethnicity composition. Boys are also slightly older than girls on average.

The next step involves estimating regression models with the dependent variable, T2 psychological distress, regressed on adverse school experiences and parental support respectively. We obtain the models with and without including the common correlates and for both the total group and by gender. The results of these models are shown in Table 2.

Table 1. Means (or proportions) and standard deviations of the variables used in the analyses (total group & by gender)

Variables	Total (N=2,905)		Boys (N=1,391)		Girls (N=1,514)		Gender Differences
	Mean	SD	Mean	SD	Mean	SD	p values
T2 psychological distress	2.87	3.06	2.26	2.53	3.43	3.39	.000
T1 psychological distress	2.80	2.93	2.39	2.58	3.18	3.18	.000
Adverse school experiences	4.01	2.80	4.38	2.87	3.66	2.69	.000
Maternal support	23.96	3.46	24.13	2.98	23.79	3.83	.011
Paternal support	22.69	4.14	23.05	3.83	22.37	4.39	.000
Antisocial behavior	3.79	4.71	4.46	5.34	3.17	3.96	.000
Parental education	5.01	1.94	5.07	1.93	4.96	1.95	.154
Intact family^	0.77	0.42	0.77	0.42	0.77	0.41	.601
Age	15.54	1.56	15.65	1.57	15.44	1.56	.001
Hispanic American^	0.11	0.31	0.11	0.31	0.11	0.31	.789
African American^	0.13	0.33	0.11	0.32	0.14	0.34	.077
Native American^	0.04	0.18	0.04	0.18	0.04	0.19	.949
Asian American^	0.05	0.22	0.05	0.22	0.05	0.21	.599

Note: ^ indicates proportions are presented.

Table 2. Independent effects of adverse school experiences and perceived parental support on T2 psychological distress with and without controlling for common correlates

Variables	Model w/o common correlates			Model with common correlates		
	Total (2,905)	Boys (1,391)	Girls (1,514)	Total (2,905)	Boys (1,391)	Girls (2,905)
Adverse school experiences	.16 (.02)***	.17 (.03)***	.22 (.04)***	.07 (.02)**	.06 (.03)*	.07 (.03)*
Maternal support	-.07 (.03)**	-.05 (.05)	-.06 (.03)*	-.01 (.02)	-.04 (.04)	.01 (.03)
Paternal support	-.18 (.03)***	-.15 (.04)***	-.18 (.04)***	-.09 (.02)***	-.08 (.04)*	-.11 (.03)***
T1 psychological distress				.41 (.03)***	.38 (.03)***	.43 (.03)***
Antisocial behavior				.07 (.02)***	.07 (.02)**	.06 (.04)+
Parental education				-.00 (.02)	.00 (.02)	-.01 (.03)
Intact family				-.05 (.02)**	-.04 (.02)*	-.05 (.03)*
Age				.01 (.01)	.06 (.02)**	-.02 (.03)
Hispanic American				.06 (.02)**	.06 (.03)*	.06 (.03)*
African American				.00 (.02)	.00 (.02)	.00 (.03)
Native American				-.01 (.02)	-.00 (.02)	.01 (.03)
Asian American				.05 (.02)**	-.00 (.01)	.10 (.03)**
Gender (girls=1)				.14 (.02)***		
Constant	-.02 (.02)	-.21 (.02)***	.18 (.03)***	-.00 (.02)	-.15 (.02)***	.12 (.03)***
R-square	.09	.11	.11	.30	.27	.29

+ $p < .10$, * $p < .05$, ** $p < .01$, *** $p < .001$ (one-tailed tests).

Table 3. Interactive effects of adverse school experiences and parental support on T2 psychological distress controlling for common correlates

Variables	Total (2,905)	Boys (1,391)	Girls (1,514)
Adverse school experiences	.06 (.02)**	.06 (.03)*	.06 (.03)*
Maternal support	-.02 (.02)	-.07 (.04)*	.01 (.03)
Paternal support	-.07 (.02)***	-.05 (.03)+	-.10 (.03)***
Adverse s. experiences x Maternal support	.03 (.03)	.06 (.04)+	.01 (.03)
Adverse s. experiences x Paternal support	-.06 (.03)*	-.07 (.04)*	-.06 (.03)*
T1 psychological distress	.41 (.03)***	.38 (.03)***	.43 (.03)***
Antisocial behavior	.07 (.02)***	.08 (.03)**	.06 (.04)+
Parental education	-.01 (.02)	.00 (.02)	-.01 (.03)
Intact family	-.05 (.02)**	-.04 (.02)*	-.05 (.03)*
Age	-.00 (.02)	.04 (.01)*	-.02 (.03)
Hispanic American	.06 (.02)**	.06 (.03)*	.06 (.03)*
African American	.00 (.02)	.00 (.02)	.00 (.03)
Native American	-.01 (.02)	-.00 (.02)	.01 (.03)
Asian American	.06 (.02)**	.00 (.01)	.10 (.03)**
Gender (girls=1)	.14 (.02)***		
Constant	-.01 (.02)	-.16 (.02)***	.12 (.03)***
R-square	.31	.28	.30

+ *p* < .10, * *p* < .05, ** *p* < .01, *** *p* < .001 (one-tailed tests).

As shown (Model I, Table 2, total group), adverse school experiences measured at T1 is related to report of psychological distress measured at T2 and this effect is positive (β = .16) and statistically significant (p < .001). Meanwhile, maternal and paternal support measured at T1 are inversely related to psychological distress at T2 respectively, but the coefficient for paternal support (β = -.18) is over twice as strong as that of maternal support (β = -.07). Further, when broken down by gender, these patterns remain similar to the total group, though the effect of maternal support is weaker and no longer significant for boys.

While the above results demonstrate that main effects of adverse school experiences and parental support on psychological distress are generally within our expectation and consistent with the literature, we do not know, however, whether adolescents who report adverse school experiences and low parental support may be distressed to begin with or are antisocial prior to having problems at school and home. Thus we estimate the same models again with prior level of psychological distress (measured at Time 1) and other common correlates added to the regression models. The results are shown in Table 2, under models with common correlates.

As shown in Table 2, with common correlates included, the regression coefficients showing adverse school experiences and parental support are much reduced, thus supporting the claim that perhaps those who are psychologically distressed or antisocial adolescents are more likely to experience adverse school experiences or problems with parenting. However, as demonstrated, even after controlling for common correlates, negative school experiences (β = .07) and paternal support (β = -.09) remain significantly related to T2 psychological distress. These patterns are similar for boys and girls. These results thus support the claims that adversities in school are salient stressor for adolescents while paternal support is an effective social resource factor against psychological problems for both boys and girls. Maternal support, however, is no longer significant over and above the influence of paternal support and after controlling for common correlates.

Of the most interest to us in the present research is whether parental support may offset (or buffer against) the impact of adverse school experiences on psychological distress and if so, which parents' support, mothers' or fathers', is more effective.

To address these questions, we estimate the final models by adding the interactive terms (i.e., adverse school experiences x maternal support, and adverse school experiences x paternal support) to the main effect models with common correlates. The results of the interactive models are presented in Table 3.

As shown in Table 3 (total group), after adding the interactive terms, the main effects of adverse school experiences and fathers' support remain the same with slight changes in the magnitude of the regression coefficients. Further, the interactive term of adverse school experiences x paternal support is negative (β = -.06) and has reached statistically significant level (p < .05). The interactive term involving mothers' support is not significant. The negative interactive effect regarding fathers' support in relation to the positive effect of adverse school experiences can be interpreted as follows: The main effect of adverse school experiences in the interactive model suggests that when fathers' support is at the mean, the effect of adverse school experiences on T2 psychological distress is β = .06. Further, when fathers' support is at 1 standard deviation (sd.) above the mean (or higher support), the effect of adverse school experiences on psychological distress is equivalent to 0 or [.06 + (-.06) x 1]. On the contrary, when fathers' support is at 1 standard deviation below the mean (lower support), the effect of adverse school experiences on psychological distress is .12 or [.06 + (-.06) x (-1)]. Apparently, high levels of paternal support offset the impact of adversities in school on psychological distress while low paternal support exacerbates the effect of adverse school experiences on psychological distress. Furthermore, this interactive effect is observed after taking into consideration of T1 psychological distress and other common correlates.

Finally, when the model is estimated separately for boys and girls, the patterns of the interactive effects remain quite similar by gender. For example, adverse school experiences predict subsequent psychological distress while controlling for earlier psychological distress and other common correlates and these effects are identical for boys and girls (i.e., β = .06 for both boys and girls). Further, fathers' support is inversely related to psychological distress, regardless of gender of the adolescent child (β = - .05 for boys and β = -.10 for girls). Finally, fathers' support reduces the effect of adverse school experiences and this observation (i.e., adverse school experiences x paternal support) is again similar for boys and girls (β = -.07 for boys and β = -.06 for girls).

However, upon closer examination of the models by gender, we notice a few changes in the regression coefficients for boys that may be worth noting: when interactive terms are added to the model (for boys), the main effect of maternal support becomes stronger (i.e., β = -.07) and reaches statistically significant level while the main effect of paternal support, β = -.05, becomes weaker than maternal support. Further, the interactive effect involving maternal support, though weak, becomes positive and statistically significant (β = .06).

Since the interactive effect is assumed to be symmetrical (Aiken and West, 1991), that is, though we assume that parental support moderates the relationship between school experiences and psychological distress, we could look at it another way by assuming adverse school experiences moderate the relationship between parental support and psychological distress. Following this rationale, we calculate the effect of maternal support on boys' psychological distress at three levels of adverse school experiences, that is, at the mean, 1sd. above the mean, and 1sd. below the mean respectively. These effects are -.01 (not significant) at 1sd. above the mean [or -.07 + (.06) x (1)], -.07 at the mean (or -.07 + (.06) x (0)), and -.13 at 1sd. below the mean [or -.07 + (.06) x (-1)] respectively. Thus these results point to the conclusion that for boys, maternal support is significantly related to psychological distress ONLY when boys experience few or no adversities in school (i.e., negative school experience at the mean or 1sd. below the mean) and the protective effect of maternal support, however, loses steam when adolescent boys encounter high levels of adversities at school.

CONCLUSION

In sum, this study yields three noteworthy findings regarding the independent and interactive effects of adverse school experiences and parental support on psychological distress among adolescents: First, adverse school experiences are significantly and positively related to report of psychological distress whereas fathers' support is inversely related to psychological distress, and these observations are made while controlling for earlier level of psychological distress and other common correlates. Further, fathers' support significantly lowers the impact of adverse school experiences on subsequent psychological distress and this effect is similar for boys and girls. Finally, mothers' support is inversely related to subsequent psychological distress only for boys who report low levels of negative experiences at school.

The significant and positive effect of adverse school experiences on psychological distress again confirms the theoretical contention that school is an important social and developmental context for adolescents (Flook and Fuligni, 2008). As suggested, difficulties or problems experienced at the school setting constitute a salient stressor that threatens to undermine adolescents' self-esteem and/or weaken their sense of school belonging (Eccles and Roeser, 2011), and in turn leading to detrimental consequences on adolescents' psychological health and emotional well-being (Cole et al., 1996; Patterson and Capaldi, 1990; Patterson and Stoolmiller, 1991). Thus, judging from the importance of school experiences, programs that aim at improving psychological health of adolescents ought to consider implementing efforts that will reduce adolescents' negative experiences at school.

Furthermore, the results show that family factors are important. Parents', especially fathers' support, serves as an important social resource that not only lowers the risk of adolescent boys and girls in general in developing poor psychological outcome. Moreover, fathers' support serves as a buffer against the impact of adversities or problems experienced by adolescents at the school setting.

Finally, although mothers' support does not seem to exert much influence over and above the effect of fathers' support, maternal support does protect adolescent boys from psychological distress under certain circumstances. In this research, we find that at least for adolescent boys who are not experiencing serious adversities at school, maternal support is related to lower levels of psychological distress independent of their prior psychological distress and other common correlates.

Our results regarding parental influence thus point to two general conclusions: Fathers' support is more important than mothers', as least in terms of protecting adolescents from developing psychological distress. This observation is consistent with studies that find importance of fathers in the lives of adolescent children (Flouri and Buchanan, 2003a, 2003b; Harris et al., 1998; Heaven et al., 2004; Kernis et al, 2000). As suggested, unlike mothers whose childcare is obligated, fathers' participation in children's lives is often a "matter of choice" (Simons and Johnson, 1996). Thus involved fathers may have a higher than average commitment to children's welfare. Also, involved fathers are more likely than mothers to play with children and the playful activities may be more beneficial to children's social and emotional development (Biller and Lopez Kimpton, 1997). Further, the beneficial effect of fathers' involvement may have encompassed the effects of some other correlates. Studies have found that marital quality or co-parental relationship is more closely related to fathers' parenting behavior than to mothers' (Belsky and Jaffee, 2006; Doherty, Kouneski, and Erickson, 1998; Furstenberg and Harris, 1992). Thus involved fathers are more likely to have been in a good relationship with mothers, which is an essential part of a healthier family environment for children. In addition, fathers who are involved usually provide financial support and thus contribute to the economic situation of the family benefitting children's growth (Crockett, Eggebeen, and Hawkings, 1993). Finally, families with involved fathers are more likely to have involved mothers too and thus double the benefits of parental involvement (Amato, 1994; Flouri, 2005).

That being said, mothers' support does exert some influence on boys, especially boys who report no or few school-related difficulties. This observation supports the contention of the opposite-sex parent-child influence such that maternal relationship with sons may help sons' emotional and psychological development, given women's general concerns over emotional connections with others (Dooley and Fedele, 2001). However, when adolescent boys are experiencing difficulties at school, maternal support may lose its effect to fathers, whose support and engagement may prove to be more effective for boys at high risk for school-related stressors.

The findings reported above, however, ought to be taken with caution due to the limitations of our data and research design. Our study is somewhat limited as we derive parental support solely from adolescent reports. While effort to study perception of parental support is legitimate and worthwhile, it is perhaps equally important to examine the actual support and involvement reported by parents themselves. Further, our data are limited to a short-time lapse between the two interviews (10 months on average). The short-time lag may not permit adequate change to occur, especially in terms of the buffering effects of parental support.

Future studies may need to replicate the findings using longitudinal data that are measured with longer time intervals (such as between 12 to 24 months). Finally, as common to longitudinal design, the present study is subject to attrition. To assess the potential biases introduced by longitudinal attrition, we conduct the analysis using data derived from Time 1 only (and thus with more adolescents present in the sample) as compared with those who are present at both Time 1 and Time 2.

The analyses based on these data, however, yield results quite consistent with the findings reported with regard to the interrelationships among the Time 1 variables. The only exception is slightly stronger coefficients reported using adolescents present in Time 1 only, thus lending to the conclusion that the results reported here may be conservative. In other words, stronger interrelationships may be observed if those who are lost to attrition are included in the study.

Despite the limitations, though, the present study fills a gap in the literature. We have gone beyond the existing research by examining whether parental support is important in offsetting the adverse psychological outcome of school adversities and which parent's support is more effective. As the study demonstrates, parental support, especially fathers', is a significant buffer against school-related difficulties among adolescents. Thus it is important to teach parents with effective parenting strategies and to encourage parental involvement, especially fathers, in the lives of adolescent children.

If these results are replicated, fathers' support is particularly important in reducing the risk of psychological distress among both boys and girls. Thus programs are needed to mobilize fathers such as by keeping the family informed of adolescent performance and experiences at school and enlisting family support, particularly fathers', in fending off the negative outcome of psychological distress.

ACKNOWLEDGMENTS

This research is based on data from the Add Health project designed by J. Richard Udry (PI) and Peter Bearman and funded by grant P01-HD31921 from the National Institute of Child Health and Human Development to the Carolina Population Center, University of North Carolina at Chapel Hill, with cooperative funding participation by the National Cancer Institute; the National Institute of Alcohol Abuse and Alcoholism; the National Institute on Deafness and Other Communication Disorders; the National Institute of Drug Abuse; the National Institute of General Medical Sciences; the National Institute of Mental Health; the National Institute of Nursing Research; the Office of AIDS Research, NIH; the Office of Behavior and Social Science Research, NIH; the Office of the Director, NIH; the Office of Research on Women's Health, NIH; the Office of Population Affairs, DHHS; the National Center for Health Statistics, Centers for Disease Control and Prevention, DHHS; the Office of Minority Health, Centers for Disease Control and Prevention, DHHS, the Office of Minority Health, Office of Public Health and Science, DHHS; the Office of the Assistant Secretary for Planning and Evaluation, DHHS; and the National Science Foundation. Persons interested in obtaining data files from the National Longitudinal Study of Adolescent Health should contact Jo Jones, Carolina Population Center, 123 West Franklin Street, Chapel Hill, NC 27516-3997 (email: jo_jones@unc.edu).

REFERENCES

Aiken, L. S. and West, S. G. (1991). *Multiple Regression: Testing and Interpreting Interactions.* Newbury Park: Sage.

Amato, P. R. (1994). Father-child relations, mother-child relations, and offspring psychological well-being in early adulthood. *Journal of Marriage and the Family, 56,* 1031–1042.

Amato, P. R. and Fowler, F. (2002). Parenting practices, child adjustment, and family diversity. *Journal of Marriage and Family, 64,* 703-716.

Anderman, E. M. (2002). School effects on psychological outcomes during adolescence. *Journal of Educational Psychology,* 94, 795-809.

Barrera, M. Jr. and Li, S. A. (1996). The relation of family support to adolescents' psychological distress and behavior problems. In G. R. Pierce and B.R. Sarason (Eds.), *Handbook of Social Support and the Family,* Plenum series on stress and coping (pp. 313–343). New York, NY, US: Plenum Press.

Baumeister, R. F. and Leary, M. R. (1995). The need to belong: Desire for interpersonal attachments as a fundamental human motivation. *Psychological Bulletin,* 117, 497–529.

Belsky, J. and Jaffee, S. R. (2006). Risk, disorder, and adaptation. In D. Cicchetti and D. J. Cohen (Eds.), *Developmental Psychopathology* (pp. 38–85), 2nd Ed., Vol. 3. Hoboken, NJ: John Wiley and Sons Inc.

Biller, H. B. and Lopez Kimpton, J. (1997). The father and the school-aged child. In M. E. Lamb (Ed.), *The Role of the Father in Child Development.* (pp. 143–161). New York: Wiley.

Burchinal, M. R., Roberts, J. E., Zeisel, S. A. and Rowley, S. J. (2008). Social risk and protective factors for African American children academic achievement and adjustment during the transition to middle school. *Developmental Psychology,* 44, 286–292.

Byrne, D. G., Davenport, S. C, and Mazanov, J. (2007). Profiles of adolescent stress: The development of the adolescent stress questionnaire. *Journal of Adolescence,* 30, 393-416.

Chipuer, H. M. (2001). Dyadic attachments and community connectedness: Links with youths' loneliness experiences. *Journal of Community Psychology,* 29, 429–446.

Cohen, S., and Wills, T. A. (1985). Stress, social support, and the buffering hypothesis. *Psychological Bulletin,* 98, 310–357.

Cole, D. A., Martin, J. M., Powers, B., and Truglio, R. (1996). Modeling causal relations between academic and social competence and depression:

A multitrait-multimethod longitudinal study of children. *Journal of Abnormal Psychology*, 105, 258–270.

Compas, B. E., Connor-Smith, J. K., Saltzman, H., Thomsen, A. H., and Wadsworth, M. E. (2001). Coping with stress during childhood and adolescence: Problems, progress, and potential in theory and research. *Psychological Bulletin*, 127, 87-127.

Cooley, C. H. (1902). *Human Nature and the Social Order*. New York: Scribner's.

Creswell, J. D., Welch, W. T., Taylor, S. E., Sherman, D. K., Gruenewald, T. L., and Mann, T. (2005). Affirmation of personal values buffers neuroendocrine and psychological stress responses. *Psychological Science*, 16, 846–851.

Crockett, L. J., Eggebeen, D. J., and Hawkings, A. J. (1993). Father's presence and young children's behavioral and cognitive adjustment. *Family Relations*, 14, 355–377.

Crosnoe, R., Erickson, K. G., and Dornbusch, S. M. (2002). Protective functions of family relationships and school factors on the deviant behavior of adolescent boys and girls: Reducing the impact of risky friendships. *Youth and Society*, 33(4), 515-544.

Doherty, W., Kouneski, E., and Erickson, M. (1998). Responsible fathering: An overview and a conceptual framework. *Journal of Marriage and the family*, 60, 277-292.

Dooley, C., and Fedele, N. (2001). Raising relational boys. In A. O'Reilley (Ed.) *Mothers and Sons: Feminism, Masculinity and the Struggle to Raise our Sons* (pp. 185-216). New York: Routledge.

DuBois D. L., and Flay, B. R. (2004). The healthy pursuit of self-esteem: comment on and alternative to the Crocker and Park 2004 formulation. *Psychological Bulletin*, 130,415–420.

Eccles, J.S. and Roeser, R.W. (2011). Schools as developmental context during adolescence. *Journal of Research on Adolescence*, 21(1), 225-241.

Eliott, D. S. and Voss, H. L. (1974). *Delinquency and the Dropout*. Lexington, MA: Lexington Books.

Flook, L. and Fuligni, A. J. (2008). Family and school spillover in adolescents' daily lives. *Child Development*, 79 (3), 776–787.

Flouri, E. (2005). Father's involvement and psychological adjustment in Indian and White British secondary school age children. *Child and Adolescent Mental Health*, 10, 32-39.

Flouri, E. and Buchanan, A. (2003a). The role of father involvement and mother involvement in adolescents' psychological well-being. *British Journal of Social Work*, 33, 399-406.

Flouri, E. and Buchanan, A. (2003b). The role of father involvement in children's later mental health. *Journal of Adolescence*, 26, 63-78.

Franke, T. M. (2000). The role of attachment as a protective factor in adolescent violent behavior. *Adolescent and Family Health* 1(1), 40-51.

Furstenberg, F. F., Jr., and Harris, K. M. (1992). The disappearing American father? Divorce and the waning significance of biological parenthood. In S. J. South and S. E. Tolnay (Eds.), *The Changing American Family: Sociological and Demographic Perspectives* (pp. 197-223). Boulder, CO: Westview Press.

Ge, X., Best, K. M., Conger, R. D., and Simons, R. L. (1996). Parenting behaviors and the occurrence and co-occurrence of adolescent depressive symptoms and conduct problems. *Developmental Psychology*, 32, 717-731.

Ge, X., Conger, R., Lorenz, F., and Simons, R. (1994). Parents' stressful life events and adolescent depressed mood. *Journal of Health and Social Behavior*, 35, 28-44.

Gecas, V., and Schwalbe, M. L. (1986). Parental behavior and adolescent self-esteem. *Journal of Marriage and Family*, 48, 37-46.

Gottfredson, M., and Hirschi, T. (1990). *A General Theory of Crime*. Stanford, CA: Stanford University Press.

Greenberg, J., Solomon, S., Pyszczynski, T., Rosenblatt, A., Burling, J., Lyon, D., Simon, L. and Pinel, E. (1992). Why do people need self-esteem? Converging evidence that self-esteem serves an anxiety-buffering function. *Journal of Personality and Social Psychology*, 63, 913-922.

Harris, J. R. (1998). *The Nurture Assumption: Why Children Turn Out the Way They Do*. New York: Free Press.

Harris, K. M., Furstenberg, F. F. JR., and Marmer, J. K. (1998). Paternal involvement with adolescents in intact families: the influence of fathers over the life course. *Demography,* 35, 201-216.

Heaven, P. C L., Newbury, K., and Mak, A. (2004). The impact of adolescent and parental characteristics on adolescent levels of delinquency and depression. *Personality and Individual Differences*, 36(1), 173-185.

Jaccard, J., Turrisi, R., and Wan, Choi K. (1990). *Interaction Effects in Multiple Regression: Quantitative Applications in the Social Sciences*. Newbury Park: Sage.

Kenny, M. E., and Barton, C. (2002). Attachment theory and research: Contributions for understanding late adolescent and young adult development. In J. Demick and C. Andreoletti (Eds.), *Handbook of Adult Development* (pp. 371-389). Norwell, MA: Kluwer.

Kernis, M. H, Brown, A. C., and Brody, G. H. (2000). Fragile self-esteem in children and its associations with perceived patterns of parent-child communication. *Journal of Personality*, 68, 225-252.

Kobak, R. R., and Sceery, A. (1988). Attachment in late adolescence: Working models, affect regulation, and representations of self and others. *Child Development*, 59, 135-146.

Lanclos, N. F. (2002). Parenting practices as a moderator of exposure to community violence. *Dissertation Abstracts International:* Section B: The Sciences and Engineering, 63(2-B), 1035.

Larson, R. and Richards, M. H. (1994). *Divergent Realities: The Emotional Lives of Mothers, Fathers, and Adolescents*. New York: Basic.

Leinonen, J. A, Solantaus, T. S, and Punamaeki, R. (2003). Parental mental health and children's adjustment: The quality of marital interaction and parenting as mediating factors. *Journal of Child Psychology and Psychiatry and Allied Disciplines*, 44(2), 227-241.

MacPhee, A. R., and Andrews, J. J. (2006). Risk factors for depression in early adolescence. *Adolescence*, 41, 435–466.

Magaro, M. M., and Weisz, J. R. (2006). Perceived control mediates the relation between parental rejection and youth depression. *Journal of Abnormal Child Psychology*, 34, 867-876.

Mario, J., and Cookston, J. T. (2007). Violent victimization, aggression, and parent-adolescent relations: Quality parenting as a buffer for violently victimized youth. *Journal of Youth and Adolescence*, 36, 635-647.

Mayhew, K. P., and Lempers, J. D. (1998). The relation among financial strain, parenting, parent self-esteem, and adolescent self-esteem. *The Journal of Early Adolescence*, 18, 145-172.

Mead, G. H. (1934). *Mind, Self and Society*. Chicago: University of Chicago Press.

Miliotis, D., Sesma, A. Jr., and Masten, A.S. (1999). Parenting as a protective process for school success in children from homeless families. *Early Education and Development,* 10(2), 111-133.

Montemayor, R. (1986). Family variation in parent-adolescent storm and stress. *Journal of Adolescent Research,* 1, 15-31.

Offer, D., Ostrov, E., and Howard, K. I. (1981). *The Adolescent: A Psychological Self-Portrait*. New York: Basic Books.

Oliver, J. M., and Paull, J. C. (1995). Self-esteem and self-efficacy; perceived parenting and family climate; and depression in university students. *Journal of Clinical Psychology*, 51, 467-448.

Orth, U., Robins, R. W., Trzesniewski, K. H., Maes, J., and Schmitt, M. (2009). Low self-esteem is a risk factor for depressive symptoms from young adulthood to old age. *Journal of Abnormal Psychology*, 118, 472-478.

Patterson, G. R., and Capaldi, D. M. (1990). A comparison of models for boys' depressed mood. In J. E.Rolf, A.Masten, D.Ciccheti, K.Neuchterlein., S.Weintaub (Eds.), *Risk and Protective Factors in the Development of Psychopathology* (pp. 141–163). Cambridge, England: Cambridge University Press.

Patterson, G. R., and Stoolmiller, M. (1991). Replications of a dual failure model for boy's depressed mood. *Journal of Consulting and Clinical Psychology*, 59, 491–498.

Pearlin, L. 1. (1989). The sociological study of stress. *Journal of Health and Social Behavior*, 30, 241-256.

Pearlin, L.I. (1995). Some conceptual perspectives on the origins and prevention of social stress. In *Socioeconomic Conditions, Stress and Mental Disorders: Toward a New Synthesis of Research and Public Policy*. http://www.mhsip.org/nimhdoc/socioeconmh_home2.htm.

Pittman, L. D., and Richmond, A. (2007). Academic and psychological functioning in late adolescence: The importance of school belonging. *Journal of Experimental Education*, 75, 270-290.

Quiery, N. (1998). Parenting and the family. In K. Trew and J. Kremer (Eds.), *Gender and Psychology* (pp. 129 -140). London: Arnold.

Repinski, D. J. and Shonk, S. M. (2002). Mothers' and fathers' behavior, adolescents' self-representations and adolescents' adjustment: A mediational model. *Journal of Early Adolescence*, 22(4), 357-383.

Roeser, R. W., Eccles, J. S., and Sameroff, A. J. (2000). School as a context of social-emotional development: A summary of research findings. *Elementary School Journal*, 100, 443–471.

Roeser, R. W., Eccles, J. S., and Strobel, K. R. (1998). Linking the study of schooling and mental health: Selected issues and empirical illustrations at the level of the individual. *Educational Psychologist*, 33, 153–176.

Sharpe, S. (1994). *Fathers and Daughters*. New York, NY: Routledge.

Shek, D. T. (2002). The relation of parental qualities to psychological well-being, school adjustment, and problem behavior in Chinese adolescents with economic disadvantage. *American Journal of Family Therapy*, 30(3), 215-230.

Simons, R. L., and Johnson, C. (1996). The impact of marital and social network support on quality of parenting. In G. R. Pierce, B. R. Sarason, and I. G. Sarason (Eds.), *Handbook of Social Support and the Family* (pp. 269 - 287). New York, NY: Plenum Press.

Starrels, M. E. (1994). Gender difference in parent-child relations. *Journal of Family Issues,* 15, 148-165.

Sui-Chu, E. H. and Willms, J. D. (1996). Effects of Parental Involvement on Eighth-Grade Achievement. *Sociology of Education*, 69 (2), 126-141.

Suldo, S. M., Shaunessy, E., Thalji, A., Michalowski, J. and Shaffer, E. (2009). Sources of stress for students in high school college preparatory and general education programs: Group differences and associations with adjustment. *Adolescence*, 44, 925-948.

Taylor, S. E. and Stanton, A. L. (2007). Coping resources, coping processes, and mental health. *Annual Review of Clinical Psychology*, 3, 377-401.

Udry, R. and Bearman, P. S. (1998). New methods for new research on adolescent sexual behavior. In R. Jessor (Ed.). *New Perspectives on Adolescent Risk Behavior* (pp. 241–269). Cambridge, UK: Cambridge University Press.

Vazsonyi, A. T. and Pickering, L. E. (2003). The importance of family and school domains in adolescent deviance: African American and Caucasian youth. *Journal of Youth and Adolescence*, 32(2), 115-128.

Vedder, P., Boekaerts, M., and Seegers, G. (2005). Perceived social support and well-being in school: The role of students' ethnicity. *Journal of Youth and Adolescence*, 34, 269–278.

Videon, T. M. (2002). The effects of parent-adolescent relationships and parental separation on adolescent well-being. *Journal of Marriage and the Family*, 64(2), 489-503.

Way, N., and Robinson, M. G. (2003). A longitudinal study of the effects of family, friends, and school experiences on the psychological adjustment of ethnic minority, low-SES adolescents. *Journal of Adolescent Research*, 18, 324–346.

Wentzel, K. R. (1998). Social relationships and motivation in middle school: The role of parents, teachers, and peers. *Journal of Educational Psychology*, 90(2), 202-209.

Wentzel, K. R. and McNamara, C. C. (1999). Interpersonal relationships, emotional distress, and prosocial behavior in middle school. *The Journal of Early Adolescence*, 19, 114–125.

Wentzel, K. R., and Watkins, D. E. (2002). Peer relationships and collaborative learning as contexts for academic enablers. *School Psychology Review*, 31, 366–377.

Whitbeck, L.B., Conger, R.D., and Kao, M.Y. (1993). The influence of parental support, depressed affect, and peers on the sexual behaviors of adolescent girls. *Journal of Family Issues*, 14(2), 261-278.

Wigfield, A., Eccles, J. S., Schiefele, U., Roeser, R., and Davis-Kean, P. (2006). Motivation. In N. Eisenberg (Ed.), *Handbook of Child Psychology*, Vol. 3, 6th ed. (pp. 933 –1002). New York, NY: Wiley.

In: Psychological Distress   ISBN: 978-1-61942-646-7
Editors: H. Ohayashi and S. Yamada   © 2012 Nova Science Publishers, Inc.

Chapter 2

PSYCHOLOGICAL DISTRESS IN ONCOLOGY

Maria Antonietta Annunziata and Barbara Muzzatti*
Centro di Riferimento Oncologico di Aviano,
National Cancer Institute, Aviano, Italy

ABSTRACT

Psychological distress in oncology expresses the emotional suffering
of patients due to cancer experience. Being diagnosed with cancer, from a
psychological point of view means facing one's vulnerability and
mortality. It also means experiencing exhausting and often painful
therapies, and living with the possibility of relapsing or, in the case of
progression, having to face new therapies. In all cases, a cancer diagnosis
abruptly interrupts patients' life programs and dramatically upsets their
daily routine. A percentage comprised between 22% and 45 % of cancer
patients show moderate or severe distress levels, that impact negatively
on the capacity to manage the disease, and on therapeutical adherence. In
this chapter, we will illustrate the psychological distress in an oncological
context, providing a longitudinal perspective to evidence the different
disease phases: from diagnosis to long-term survivorship or terminality.
We will then attempt to determine the principal socio-demographic and
clinical variables related to psychological distress. Being a "familiar
disease", cancer affects the caregivers' well-being, too: in this chapter,

* Address for correspondence: Dr.ssa M. A. Annunziata, Unit of Oncological Psychology, Centro
di Riferimento Oncologico, IRCCS Istituto Nazionale Tumori, Via F. Gallini, 2, 33080
Aviano (PN), Italy. Tel. +39/0434/659258; Fax: +39/0434/652182. e-mail:
annunziata@cro.it

the patterns of distress in oncological patients caregivers will be examined. Finally, the most common assessment tools for psychological distress used in oncology will be illustrated, along with some useful indications for its management.

INTRODUCTION

In the collective imagination, cancer is still often associated with death. Thanks to the diffusion of screening practice (e.g. pap test, mammography, fecal occult blood test), to medical and technological development, (e.g. newer drugs, surgical techniques and therapeutic protocols) together with healthier behaviours (primary prevention) induced by informative campaigns (against harmful effects of smoke, alcohol, lack of exercise and fat rich diet) cancer is now becoming a chronic pathology, but still remains a serious disease. It requires demanding therapies that place considerable strain on the body and psyche.

Pain, fatigue, infertility, amputations, functional damage to the organs involved, are only some of the effects of treatments that may occur in the acute phase of disease, or after the end of treatments or even later. Moreover, these effects are not just physical and limited to the organ involved but could have repercussions on the emotional asset, well-being and quality of life.

Besides these aspects, there are more strictly psychosocial states and symptoms, consequent to the objective conditions imposed by the disease (hospitalisation, isolation, discontinuation of patients' routine and individual projects) and to the subjective meaning patients attribute to cancer and to the fact of having developed it.

From a psychological point of view, cancer is a traumatic and stressful event (Kelly, Smithers, Swanson, McLeod, Thomson, & Walpole, 1995; Green, Rowland, Krupnick, Ebstein, Stockton, Stern, Spertus, & Steakley, 1998; Erickson & Steiner, 2000). It was observed that like in other personal experiences that may break abruptly into someone's life, menacing his/her incolumity, also in the oncological experience it can be observed that there is the onset of an emotional crisis followed by a painful process of psychosocial adaptation/clearing of the trauma.

The definition "psychological distress" (or "emotional distress") includes all the psychoemotional aspects related to cancer that may undermine the coping with the disease and the therapeutical adherence. Cancer is a long disease progress: it is, therefore, difficult to speak of "healing" even many years after the diagnosis and the end of treatment. This is why we usually talk about "long-term cancer survivorship". In Italy it was established that patients free from disease and treatments for at least five years can be considered the long-term survivors (Simonelli, Annunziata, Chimenti, Berretta, & Tirelli, 2008; Simonelli, Berretta, Tirelli, & Annunziata, 2008). In this phase, follow-up checks and the progression of the disease or its relapse are events that stimulate emotionally patients and that may consequently trigger further psychological distress.

Cancer is also described as a family disease (Weihs & Reiss, 1996; Annunziata, 2003): the structure and the family dynamics are affected from the disease of one of its members. Each member involved in caregiving, has to face the suffering caused by the fear of separation, and death of their relative. Family members also have to confront their own vulnerability with respect to disease (in general, not just oncological) and death. The psychological distress, then, interferes with the whole family well-being and quality of life.

In the present chapter, we will present the psychological distress as a consequence of cancer. We will describe its manifestations and prevalence also referring to the different stages of the disease trajectory and to the principal socio-demographic and clinical variables related. Moreover, we will illustrate the assessment methods more frequently employed in oncology, along with useful indications for its management. Finally, we will discuss the psychological distress in cancer patients' caregivers.

DEFINITION, MANIFESTATIONS AND PREVALENCE

The first tentative to assess and manage the psychological and psychosocial consequences of cancer was made by the National Comprehensive Cancer Network (NCCN). In 1997, a multidisciplinary group comprising psychiatrists, psychologists, oncologists, nurses, social operators, patients' representatives was set up to establish the first set of clinical practice standards and guidelines for the assessment and management of distress in cancer patients (Holland, 1997). These guidelines were published for the first time in 1999 and are updated annually.

In order to avoid the stigmatizing terms of "psychiatric", or "psychosocial", the word "distress" was chosen to define "a multifactorial unpleasant emotional experience of a psychological (cognitive, behavioral, emotional), social, and/or spiritual nature that may interfere with the ability to cope effectively with cancer, its physical symptoms and its treatment. Distress extends along a continuum, ranging from common normal feelings of vulnerability, grief and fears, to problems that can become disabling, such as depression, anxiety, panic, social isolation, and existential and spiritual crisis [...]" (NCCN, 1999). The adjective "psychological" defines this personal state, conferring an emotional, relational, social and existential content starting from the body disease.

Considering the sudden, pervasive and demanding nature of cancer, it is not surprising that patients may experience feelings of grief, uncertainty, preoccupation, demoralization, fear, anxiety, and/or anger. Recognizing and monitoring psychological distress means monitoring emotions and eventually intervene so that they do not become chronic, thus crippling and interfering with psychosocial functioning and/or result in full-blown psychopathology (van't Spijker, Trijsburg, & Duivenvoorden, 1997; Holland & Alici, 2010). Several studies have demonstrated that clinically significant distress is associated with maladaptive coping, reduction in quality of life, impairment in social relationships, risk of suicide, longer rehabilitation phase, poor adherence to treatment, abnormal illness behaviour, family dysfunction, psychosocial morbidity, and possibly shorter survival (Ballenger, Davidson, Lecrubier, Nutt, Jones, & Berard, 2001; Grassi & Riba, 2009; Hamer, Chida, & Molloy, 2009; Bringman, Singer, Höckel, Stolzenburg, Krauss, & Schwarz, 2008): these are additional reasons in favour of regular monitoring and timely treatment of distress.

In 2006 Bultz and Carlson summarized the necessities and the value of monitoring emotional distress and defined it the "sixth vital sign" in oncology, along with temperature, respiration, heart rate, blood pressure and pain: "supported emotional distress as the sixth vital sign implying that monitoring of emotional distress is as vital an indicator of a patient's state of being, needs and progress through the disease, as are the other vital signs" (Butz & Carlson, 2006). The centrality of distress as the sixth vital sign was later relaunched by the International Psycho-Oncology Society (IPOS) in June 2009.

In the presence of the diagnosis of cancer, then, feelings of fear, sadness, anxious and depressive states, symptoms that refer to anxiety, depressive and adjustment disorders may build up psychological distress. Even if responding to established criteria for the psychiatric diagnosis, they are considered the manifestation of the condition of a crisis caused by the disease as a stressful and traumatizing event (Società Italiana di Psico-Oncologia, 1998).

In relation with the manifestations of psychological distress in oncology, it must be remembered that some symptoms pertinent to depression and/or anxiety – like, for ex. asthenia, troubled sleeping, lack of appetite - are sometimes side effects of treatments: it is then necessary to make an accurate differential analysis to avoid any erroneous evaluation and attribution.

In North America and Western Europe, the prevalence of psychological distress is comprised between 22% and 45% (Zabora, Binzzenhofeszoc, Burbow, Hooker, & Piantadosi, 2001; Carlson & Bultz, 2003; Carlson, Angen, Cullum, Goodey, Koopmans, Lamont, MacRae, Martin, Pelletier, Robinson, Simpson, Speca, Tillotson, & Bultz, 2004; Keller, Sommerfeldt, Fischer, Knight, Riesbeck, Löwe, Herfarth, & Lehnert, 2004; Gil, Grassi, Travado, Tomamichel, & Gonzalez, 2006; Pasquini, Biondi, Costantini, Cairoli, Ferrarese, Picadi, & Sternberg, 2006; Sellick & Edwardson, 2007; Strong, Waters, Hibberd, Rush, Cargill, Storey, Walker, Wall, Fallon, & Sharpe, 2007; Dolbeault, Bredart, Mignot, Hardy, Gauvain-Piquard, Mandereau, Asselain, & Medioni, 2008). The lower percentage was registered in Great Britain, the higher in Southern Europe (Italy, Spain, Portugal).

The two more studied aspects of psychological distress are anxiety and depression: depressive states prevalence is comprised between 9% and 21% (Keller et al., 2004; Gil et al., 2006; Strong et al., 2007; Iconomou, Iconomou, Argyriou, Nikolopoulos, Ifanti, & Kalofonos, 2008; Annunziata, Muzzatti, Bidoli, & Veronesi, in press), anxiety prevalence was comprised between 10% and 48% (Keller et al., 2004; Gil et al., 2006; Strong et al., 2007; Iconomou et al., 2008; Annunziata et al. in press; Stark & Housel, 2000; Stark, Kiely, Smith, Velikova, House, & Selby, 2002).

The reasons that may explain the wide range that comprises the psychological distress values and those of its anxious and depressive components, are personal data (for example, gender or age) and cultural factors related to the tendency to share one's own personal experiences. The different values may also be influenced by the stage and type of disease, the different treatment facility of referral (for ex. ward or outpatients clinic/office), the way the data collection was conducted (for ex. interview or self-filling questionnaire), or type of assessing tool employed.

PSYCHOLOGICAL DISTRESS ALONG THE DISEASE TRAJECTORY

Cancer experience can be divided into phases: diagnostic, therapeutic, remission and follow-up, long-term survivorship, progression and terminality (Annunziata & Muzzatti, in press). The diagnosis of a severe disease like cancer allows certainty about a current pathological phase that paradoxically gives way to a series of uncertainties about life perspective, efficacy of treatments, side effects and prognosis.

To obtain a diagnosis of cancer is not usually a "punctual" fact. Generally, the diagnosis is the outcome of a long process of tests, exams and consultations with different specialists whose outcomes are awaited by patients in uncertainty.

Even undergoing an oncological treatment means facing insecurity: about the efficacy of the cure and, more often, about its efficacy extent (from a temporary remission of symptoms to the complete healing). Cancer treatments may have instant, long-term or late side effects: they are often severe, and are differently tolerated from patient to patient. Sometimes they also need some adjustments along the trajectory of the treatment. In this phase, even possible permanent side effects (the most severe are infertility and disability) could preoccupy the patients, who fear the possible future considerable reduction of their physical activity and quality of life: these worries causes concern and a sense of suspension. One of the primary variables that allow clinicians to understand patients' personal experiences in this phase is the individual significance that each patient gives to side effects and treatment-induced limitations (whether concurrent with treatments, or as late side effects).

At the end of the treatments, doctors may welcome therapy outcomes (for ex. a reduction of cancer lump) as a success, while often patients cannot fully appreciate the therapy results. This is due to the side effects, that can endure (thus limiting patients' quality of life and well-being), and to the concern about these effects or of a possible relapse. In particular, the period that precedes or follows the follow-ups is particularly anxiety-inducing and is full of concerns about one's health. In this phase, it is more probable that patients develop concern and worry about the possibility that their descendants (real or potential) may develop cancer, too.

Emotional disorders, anxious and depressive personal experiences and preoccupations may persist for a long time (or they may set in later), thus characterizing also the long-term cancer survivorship phase.

From an emotional point of view, the relapse is usually more severe than the diagnosis, because it triggers other emotions and states of mind, like impotence, defeat, abandonment, ambivalence, impossibility to trust again and incapacity. These are common emotions when facing a failure (and the relapse is considered as such), it is, therefore, frequent for patients to experience and express them.

Finally, becoming terminally ill may foster a sense of failure, depression, loss, impotence and abandonment: these emotional and complex activities constitute the psychological distress.

Psychological distress seems not to change substantially along the disease continuum (Osborne, Elsworth, & Hopper, 2003; Annunziata, Muzzatti, & Bidoli, 2011), except for the advanced and terminal phases (Zabora et al., 2001; Iconomou et al., 2008; Herschbach, Book, Brandl, Keller, Lindena, Neuwöhner, & Marten-Mittag, 2008). Patients who obtain the diagnosis in an advanced stage of disease show higher distress, especially the presence of metastasis (Herschbach, Keller, Knight, Brandl, Huber, Henrich, & Marten-Mittag, 2004). Moreover, distress is higher when the disease is active rather than in the remission phase (Carlson et al., 2004; Strong et al., 2007), but still may, as reported before, characterize also the long-term survivorship phase (Annunziata, Muzzatti, Bianchet, Berretta, Chimienti, Lleshi, & Tirelli, 2009).

ADDITIONAL CLINICAL DISTRESS-RELATED PSYCHOLOGICAL FACTORS

As far as aggressiveness, curability, and prognosis are concerned, neoplasias are not all the same. In fact, not all organs possibly involved in cancer are not essential for survival and may have different symbolic significance, functionality for an acceptable quality of life and prosthesization. Treatments do not have the same tolerability, side effects consequences nor efficacy. Many clinical variables (among which disease stage, good general state of health, and comorbidity) concur in determining psychological distress in oncological patients. Therefore, distress seems to be associated with the type of diagnosis: its prevalence, in fact, is higher in lung cancer (43.4%), in cerebral tumors, Hodgkin and non-Hodgkin lymphomas, head and neck, pancreas and breast cancers, leukemia, melanomas, colon's, prostate's, and gynecologic cancers patients (29.6%) (Zabora et al., 2001); it is higher in breathing system and gynecological tumors (Herschbach et al., 2008); in breast and soft tissue tumors (Herschbach et al., 2004) (see also: Carlson et al., 2004).

The most distress-related treatment is chemotherapy, while patients report radiotherapy and surgery to be as stressful as not being treated at all (Herschbach et al., 2008).

Anxiety is more intense and wide-spread among lung cancer patients, whereas depression is more prevalent in lung and breast cancers (Sellick & Edwardson, 2007). Nevertheless, in a recent study by Annunziata et al. (in press) no associations were found between either anxious or depressive state and cancer survival (i.e. cancers for which the survival rating after 5 years is less than 50% [e.g. lung or stomach cancer] vs. cancers for which the survival rating after 5 years is higher than 50% [e.g. breast or prostate cancer]), disease phase (diagnostic = within 1 month since diagnosis; therapeutic = 3-6 months since diagnosis), ongoing and planned treatments.

SOCIO-DEMOGRAPHIC-ASSOCIATED FACTORS

Psychological distress seems to be associated also with socio-demographic factors along with clinical factors. In particular, distress seems to be higher in women with respect to men (e.g.: Strong et al., 2007; Dolbeault et al., 2008; Iconomou et al., 2008; Herschbach et al., 2004, 2008), even though Carlson et al. (2004), for example, did not report gender-related differences. It also seems to be more common in younger patients (Osborne et al., 2003; Herschbach et al., 2004; Strong et al., 2007). Moreover, according to Iconomous et al. (2008), patients who do not have a partner (i.e. singles, divorced, widowed) show more psychological distress respect partnered patients (these data were not confirmed by Herschbach et al., 2004).

The data on the two main components of psychological distress are less univocal. Depression is reported as gender-associated (higher values in women by Carlson et al., 2004 but as non gender-related by Sellick & Edwardson (2007) e by Annunziata et al. (in press); as age-related (higher in older patients) by Sellick & Edwardson (2007), but not by Annunziata et al. (in press); higher values were found by Sellick & Edwardson (2007) in widowers, while Annunziata et al. (in press) reported no marital-status dependent variations. As regards anxiety, Sellick & Edwardson (2007) and Annunziata et al. (in press) reported higher values in women, while Carlson et al. did not endorse these data (2004); while, differently from Annunziata et a. (in press) Sellick & Edwardson (2007) reported an association between both anxiety state and age and anxiety and marital status.

Moreover, further risk factors seem to be worse physical functioning, pain, fatigue, previous psychiatric disorders, bad communication between patients and therapeutic team and lack of social support (Ballenger et al., 2001; Stark et al., 2002; Lueboonthavatchai, 2007; Dolbeault et al., 2008). Personal or familiar cancer history were associated with higher distress (Rabin, Rogers, Pinto, Nash, Frierson, & Trask, 2007).

ASSESSING PSYCHOLOGICAL DISTRESS

If psychological distress is a *vital sign* in oncology as well as temperature, respiration, heart rate, blood pressure and pain it must be likewise monitored and treated along the entire disease process (Bultz & Carlson, 2006; NCCN, 2011). It is then necessary to identify tools that combine the necessary psychometric properties (validity, reliability, sensitivity) - that make it a useful and informative instrument- with rapidity of administration and good understandability: the qualities that make this instrument manageable in a context already overloaded with tasks, and acceptable by often debilitated patients. Moreover, if the aim is identifying oncological patients at risk of developing psychiatric disorders or presenting a compromised therapeutic adherence (and consequently a compromised therapeutical efficacy), screening tools seem to be more adapt than assessment tools, since they are rapid, usually self-report, allow to prospectively identify patients who could more probably suffer from psychological distress. Assessment tools in general take longer to be administered, require more specific competences from administrators and could then be used by trained personnel for a further diagnostic examination (second-level screening).

In 2009 Vodermaier, Linden and Siu published a comprehensive review on emotional distress assessment tools in oncology, listing as many as 33 instruments. In 2010, Luckett, Butow, King, Oguchi, Heading, Hackl, Rankin, & Price listed 30 different distress, anxiety and depression assessment instruments to be used for assessing psychosocial interventions in English-speaking adult oncological patients. Finally, in the same year, Mitchell identified 45 short and ultrashort tools (i.e. tools with fewer than 14 items that require less than 5 minutes to complete) to be employed in assessing psychological distress. Most of the tools listed in these three studies have fast administration and scoring, and are feasible. However, as the authors themselves have highlighted, only for a small percentage of tools we have sufficient data to assess the required psychometric properties. In Table, 1 we list as an example (with no claim of being exhaustive) of the psychological distress assessment tools commonly recommended in oncological contexts.

In table 1, the big heterogeneity of item numbers and particularly of the dimensions investigated by the different instruments is evident. The principles that should help in choosing a tool are the (clinical or research) aims, the degree of prostration, the eventual use of other assessment tools at the same time and the existence of a tool adaptation to the cultural/national environment where the it would be used.

Table 1. Main screening tools recommended by the international literature for detecting emotional distress in oncology

Tool	Authors	Number of Items	Investigated Dimensions
Beck Depression Inventory (BDI)	Beck, Ward, Mendelson, Mock, & Erbaugh (1961)	21	Depression
Brief Symptom Inventory-18 (BSI-18)	Derogatis (2000)	18	Clinically relevant psychological symptoms (anxiety, depression, somatization)
Center for Epidemiologic Studies Depression Scale (CES-D)	Radloff (1977)	20	Depression
Combined Depression Questions	Akechi, Okuyama, Sugawara, Shima, Furukawa, & Uchitomi (2006)	2	Depressive disorders
Distress Thermometer and Problem Checklist (DT+PC)	NCCN (2003)	1+38	General emotional distress + problems (practical, family, physical, emotional, spiritual)
Edinburgh Postnatal Depression Scale (EPDS)	Cox, Holden, & Sagovsky (1987)	10	Depressive symptoms
Edinburgh Postnatal Depression Scale, brief version (BEDS)	Lloyd-Williams, Shiels, & Dowrick (2007)	6	Depressive symptoms
General Health Questionnaire 28 (GHQ-28)	Goldberg (1972)	28	Psychological distress
General Health Questionnaire 12 (GHQ-12)	Goldberg (1972)	12	Psychological distress

Tool	Authors	Number of Items	Investigated Dimensions
Hospital Anxiety and Depression Scale (HADS)	Zigmond & Snaith (1983)	14	Psychological distress/Anxiety and depressive symptoms in medical settings
Psychological Distress Inventory (PDI)	Morasso, Costantini, Baracco, Borreani, & Capelli, (1996)	13	Psychological distress
Psychosocial Screen for Cancer (PSSCAN)	Linden, Yi, Barroetavena, MacKenzie, & Doll (2005)	21	Depressive symptoms, anxiety symptoms, quality of life (global), quality of life (number of days impaired), perceived social support, social support desired
Questionnaire on Stress in Cancer Patients – Revised (QSCP-r23)	Herschbac, Marten-Mittag, & Henrich (2003)	23	Psychosomatic symptoms, anxiety, information gaps, impairments in everyday life, social distress
Rotterdam Symptom Checklist (RSCL)	de Haes, van Knippenberg, & Neijt (1990)	30+8+1	Psychological and physical distress + daily activities and 1 item on today's, quality of life

PSYCHOLOGICAL DISTRESS MANAGEMENT

Even though the literature reports that about 20-40% of oncological patients experiences significant distress levels (Derogatis, Morrow, Fetting, Penman, Piasetsky, Schmale, Henrichs, & Carnicke, 1983), distress is recognized and reported to mental health services only in less than 10% of cases (Kadan-Lottick, Vanderwerker, Block, Zhang, & Prigerson, 2005). Unrecognized distress implies some issues, both for patients (on how to make therapeutical decisions and adhere to treatments, book further visits), and for the oncological team (stress, and time spent in medical examinations) (Zabora, 1998; Carlson & Bultz, 2003; NCCN, 2011). There are important evidences that psychosocial, behavioral and pharmacological interventions may reduce distress and improve patients' capacity to understand and adhere to treatments, thus ameliorating medical care results (Adler, 2008; Jacobsen, 2009). As mentioned above, the National Comprehensive Cancer Network has developed distress management guidelines for identification, assessment and treatment of distress. Among the standard activities of distress managing, NCCN recommends a regular monitoring of the type and amount of distress from the first visit on, especially in change of state of the disease. NCCN also recommends a fast treatment of distress in all disease stages, the development of educational training for healthcare operators and the presence of health professionals specifically qualified on psychosocial aspects of cancer as part of the staff or a point of reference. As defined by the NCCN "Distress, extends along a continuum, ranging from common normal feelings of vulnerability, sadness, and fears to problems that can become disabling, such as depression, anxiety, panic, social isolation, and existential and spiritual crisis": treating psychological distress, then, must consider its intensity as well as its quality.

Mild distress usually comprises symptoms like fear, worries, uncertainty about the future; anger; fear on losing control on one's life; troubles in sleeping, eating, concentrating; negative thinking. Communication can help the revelation/elaboration of patients' emotions when it is based on active listening, and includes open questions and emotional words, responds appropriately to patients' emotional cues, and has a patient-centered consulting style (Ryan, Schofield, Cockburn, Butow, Tattersall, Turner, Girgis, Bandaranayake, & Bowman, 2005).

Moderate or severe distress includes more intense and enduring symptoms: worries and fears, sadness and depression, many forms of anxiety-depressive disorders, adjustment disorder and even severe familiar problems and spiritual crisis. In this case, the oncological staff, according with the severeness and distress type (detected by screening tools) evaluates the possibility of addressing patients to the adapter health professional (psychologist, psychiatrist, social worker, spiritual counselor). In any case, the presence of moderate/severe distress requires further evaluation (assessment or second level screening) considering patients behaviors, psychic symptoms, psychiatric history, drug use, pain management and further physical symptoms, body image and sexuality, familiar and social support and decision-making ability.

If the nature of distress is prevalently psychological –disease adaptation, coping or communicative abilities, difficulties in accepting physical or functional changes (e.g. body image, sexuality), difficulties in decision-making – the interventions resulting effective in reducing stress and in ameliorating the quality of life include problem solving, some interventions on the crisis, individual and familiar psychotherapies, support and group psychotherapy, cognitive behavioral therapy (CBT). The latter has proved effective in alleviating psychological (anxiety, depression) and physical (pain, fatigue) symptoms, even consequent to medical procedures (NCCN, 2011; Moorey & Greer, 1997; Gielissen, Verhagen, & Bleijenberg, 2007).

If the nature of the distress is prevalently psychosocial (comporting social isolation; practical problems like transportation issues, daily life activities, work/school; financial issues; caregiver unavailability etc.), patients must be addressed to social welfare.

In case patients experience problems of a spiritual/religious kind, they may be addressed to a spiritual counselor.

In case there are some psychiatric symptoms – guilt, desperation, depressive disorders, suicidal thoughts, adjustment disorders, anxiety disorders, post-traumatic stress disorders- patients have to be evaluated by a psychiatrist and must undergo a specific psychopharmacological treatment (NCCN, 2011). The literature suggest that anti-anxiety and anti-depressive drugs are effective in treating anxiety and depression in adult oncological patients (Jacobsen, Donovan, Zöe, & Watson, 2006; Pirl, 2004; Williams & Dale, 2006).

The identification of patients psychosocial needs is crucial to develop a program of needs managing. IOM report (Adler, 2008) supported NCCN work on distress management guidelines, proposing a model that should be implemented in oncology practice for an efficient development of a psychosocial health service. The program should include a screening for distress and psychosocial needs; the creation of a treatment plan, to address these needs; the creation of a referral system to services as needed for psychosocial care; and a reevaluation as appropriate.

Screening and distress early identification allows, then, an effective psychological distress management and facilitates medical management.

PSYCHOLOGICAL DISTRESS IN CANCER PATIENTS CAREGIVERS

Medical progress is making hospitalization time shorter, and cancer is more frequently regarded as a *chronic* disease: as a consequence, nowadays, it is often a relative or a friend who takes charge of providing caring services to cancer patients. Unfortunately, these carers frequently do not have technical competencies, nor have they had any adequate psychological training (Zwahlen, Hagenbuch, Carley, Recklitis, & Buchi, 2008; Pitceathly & Maguire, 2003). They are also too emotionally involved with patients.

The terms "caregivers" or "carers" describe who is primarily involved in assisting a sick person. Carers are usually close relatives (the spouse or children in case of older patients) and occasionally some friends. The assistance they can give usually is nonprofessional: it is usually provided because of the affective relationship they have with the sick person or for the closeness to patients. Caring for oncological patients entails assistance in administering drugs or medications, giving meals, helping in maintaining patients' personal hygiene, giving practical and emotional support during hospitalization and home care, listening and providing emotional closeness. All these tasks bring about an emotional overload, routine changes and additional tasks to carers' daily life. In the literature, the impact of discase on relatives and caregivers is called "burden": taking an interest in the psychological distress of carers means dealing with the psychological component of burden that also involves economical aspects, life schedule and social life changes.

A percentage comprised between 20% and 30% of caregivers show psychological distress. In case patients have advanced cancer or have to undergo palliative care, the percentage of caregivers that show psychological distress increases to 50%-60% (Pitceathly & Maguire, 2003; Hodges, Humphris, & Macfarlane, 2005; Dumont, Turgeon, Allard, Gagnon, Charbonneau, & Vézina, 2006; McLean & Jones, 2007). As the disease progresses, in fact, caregiving may become increasingly hard and demand more commitment from the caregivers (e.g. giving night assistance); at the same time, carers' worries about the progression of the disease grow. Psychological distress is higher if patients experience pain or a low-performance status, as well as in case the caregivers have their own health problems (Pitceathly & Maguire, 2003; Dumont et al., 2006; Matthews, Baker, & Spillers, 2003).

In general, the sociodemografic variables that seem to be mostly associated with psychological distress are the gender (with higher levels of distress in women than in men), having had a previous history of affective disorders, and being the partner of the sick person (Pitceathly & Maguire, 2003). Furthermore, caregiving requires changes in one's social role and causes disruptions in daily life. The lack of formal (e.g. information by medical staff) and informal support may cause higher psychological distress in carers as well (Pitceathly & Maguire, 2003; Matthews et al., 2003; Dumont et al., 2006).

Comparing psychological distress in 135 oncological patients and their own caregivers, Matthews (2003) observed that caregivers means on overall psychological distress were significantly higher than those shown for patients, and that there are gender differences among caregivers (women reported higher distress), but not among patients. When the sick persons' caregivers are also their partners (this is the most studied pattern), it seems that gender is more associated with psychological distress than the status/position of being the care provider or the recipient of treatments (Hagedoorn, Sanderman, Bolks, Tuinstra, & Coyne, 2008).

Since caregivers report having the same stress levels as patients, the association between patients' and caregivers' distress (Hodges et al., 2005) and the prolonged assistance tasks presently required by cancer care to caregivers, suggest the importance of monitoring the psychological distress in caregivers as well.

CONCLUSION

Cancer presents itself as a pervasive, multifaceted experience of suffering. Very frequently, it is not limited to the body part involved in the disease: the experience of suffering regards the whole organism, and the psychological and social spheres, too. Both systemic treatments (like chemotherapy) and localized therapies (surgery and radiotherapy), may cause side effects in organs and distal systems; analogously, the psychoemotional asset and socio-relational functioning resent, for short or longer periods, of disease. The expression "psychological distress", is "extensive on purpose, and being far from stigmatizing terms belonging to psychiatry, it wishes to encompass all forms of disease consequent to cancer experience, whether mild and temporary or severe. Therefore, the psychosocial treatment has been considered as a quality fundamental aspect of cancer care (Adler, 2008) and, in particular, regular monitoring and consequent psychological distress management are amply recommended (NCCN).

However, patients are reluctant in revealing their psychological problems to oncologists. The words *psychological, psychiatric,* and *emotional* are as stigmatizing as cancer. Consequently, patients do not talk about their distress with physicians. Physicians, in turn, do not ask patients about their psychological worries (NCCN, 2011). Besides, patients often avoid presenting their own emotional or quality of life issues, as if these problems were the right price to pay for their healing; on the other side, the chronic lack of time and the poor qualifications (probably more self-attributed than objective) of medical and nursing personnel to deal with psycho-emotional issues, induce in overlooking them. Body and mind are not two opposed entities mutually excluding each other: on the contrary, they constitute a person in its whole, and are to be considered both in health and in illness. It is, therefore, necessary for patients to be led to understand this interconnection and to be stimulated in taking care of both. At the same time, medical and nursing personnel, usually educated in curing the body, must also be trained in recognizing, welcoming, managing the emotional aspects. Formation and information represent, then, the first step for recognizing forms of impairment to well-being and to the highest possible quality of life in patients and survivors, and consequently to treatments, too. Patients and caregivers should be informed of the existence of this multidimensional standard, and that they have the right to request it in oncological clinical practice. Health operators should be trained and supervised in communication and efficient (personal and patients') emotion management. Multidisciplinarity in therapeutical équipes must thus become an effective and concrete reality in a total medical care.

REFERENCES

Adler, N.E. (2008). *Cancer care for the whole patient: meeting psychosocial health needs*. Institute of Medicine (IOM). eds. Washington, DC: The National Academies Press.

Akechi, T., Okuyama, T., Sugawara, Y., Shima, Y., Furukawa, T.A., & Uchitomi, Y. (2006). Screening for depression in terminally ill cancer patients in Japan. *Journal of Pain Symptom Management, 31*(1), 5-12.

Annunziata, M.A. (2003). La famiglia e il cancro. In M.L. Bellani,L., G. Morasso, D. Amadori, W. Orrù, L. Grassi, P.G. Casali, P. Bruzzi (Eds.), *Psiconcologia* (pp. 301-305). Milano: Masson.

Annunziata, M.A., & Muzzatti, B. (in press). Improving communication efectiveness in oncology: The role of emotion. In A. Surbone M. Zwitter, M. Rajer, R. Stiefel (Eds.), *New Challenges in Communication with Cancer Patients*. Springer.

Annunziata, M.A., Muzzatti, B., Bianchet, K., Berretta, M., Chimienti, E., Lleshi, A., & Tirelli, U. (2009). Sopravvivere al cancro: una rassegna sulla qualità di vita nella cancer survivorship. *Psicologia della Salute*, 10(3), 55-71.

Annunziata, M.A., Muzzatti, B., & Bidoli, E. (2011). Psychological distress and needs of cancer patients: a prospective comparison between the diagnostic and the therapeutic phase. *Supportive Care in Cancer, 19*(2), 291-295.

Annunziata, M.A., Muzzatti, B., Bidoli, E., & Veronesi, A. (in press). Emotional distress and needs in Italian cancer patients: prevalence and associations with socio-demographic and clinical factors. *Tumori.*

Ballenger, J.C., Davidson, J.R.T., Lecrubier, Y., Nutt, D.J., Jones, R.D., & Berard, R.M.F.; International Consensus Group on Depression and Anxiety (2001). Consensus statement on depression, anxiety and oncology. *Journal of Clinical Psychiatry, 62*(suppl. 8), 64-67.

Beck, A.T., Ward, C.H., Mendelson, M., Mock, J., & Erbaugh, J. (1961). An inventory for measuring depression. *Archives of General Psychiatry, 4*(6), 561-571.

Bringman, H., Singer, S., Höckel, M., Stolzenburg, J.U., Krauss, O., & Schwarz, R. (2008). Longitudinal analysis of psychiatric morbidity in cancer patients. *Onkologie*, 31, 343-344.

Bultz, B.D., & Carlson, L.E. (2006). Emotional distress: the sixth vital sign — future directions in cancer care. *Psycho-Oncology, 15*, 93-95.

Carlson, L.E., Angen, M., Cullum, J., Goodey, E., Koopmans, J., Lamont, L., MacRae, J.H., Martin, M., Pelletier, G., Robinson, J., Simpson, J.S., Speca, M., Tillotson, L., & Bultz, B.D. (2004). High levels of untreated distress and fatigue in cancer patients. *British Jorunal of Cancer, 14*;90(12), 2297-2304.

Carlson, L.E., & Bultz, B.D. (2003). Cancer distress screening. Needs, models, and methods. *Journal of Psychosomatic Research, 55*, 403-409.

Cox, J.L., Holden, J.M., & Sagovsky, R. (1987). Detection of postnatal depression. Development of the 10-item Edinburgh Postnatal Depression Scale. *British Journal of Psychiatry, 150*(6), 782-786.

Derogatis, L.R. (2000). *BSI-18: administration, scoring and procedures manual.* Minneapolis, MN: National Computer Systems.

Derogatis, L.R., Morrow, G.R., Fetting, J., Penman, D., Piasetsky, S., Schmale, A.M., Henrichs, M., & Carnicke, C.L.M. Jr. (1983). The prevalence of psychiatric disorders among cancer patients. *Journal of the American Medical Association, 249*, 751-757.

Dolbeault, S., Bredart, A., Mignot, V., Hardy, P., Gauvain-Piquard, A., Mandereau, L., Asselain, B., & Medioni, J. (2008). Screening for psychological distress in two French cancer centers: feasibility and performance of the adapted distress thermometer. *Palliative Supportive Care, 6*(2), 107-117.

Dumont, S., Turgeon, J., Allard, P., Gagnon, P., Charbonneau, C., & Vézina, L. (2006). Caring for a loved one with advanced cancer: determinants of psychological distress in family caregivers. *Journal of Palliative Medicine, 9*(4), 912-921.

Erickson, S.Y., & Steiner, H. (2000). Trauma spectrum adaptation somatic symptoms in long-term pediatric cancer survivors. *Psychosomatics, 41*(4).

Gil, F., Grassi, L., Travado, L., Tomamichel, M., & Gonzalez, J.R.; Southern European Psycho-Oncology Study Group (2006). Use of distress and depression thermometers to measure psychosocial morbidity among southern European cancer patients. *Supportive Care in Cancer, 13*(8), 600–606.

Goldberg, D. (1972). *The detection of psychiatric illness by questionnaire.* London: Oxford University Press.

Grassi, L., & Riba, M. (2009). New frontiers and challenges of psychiatry in oncology and palliative care. In G.N. Christodoulou, M. Jorge, J.E. Mezzich (Eds.), *Advances in psychiatry* (vol 3, pp 105-114). Athens: Beta Medical.

Green, B.L., Rowland, J.H., Krupnick, J.L., Ebstein, S.A., Stockton, P., Stern, N.M., Spertus, I.L., & Steakley, C. (1998). Prevalence of posttraumatic stress disorder in women with breast cancer. *Psychosomatic Medicine, 39*(2), 102-111.

de Haes, J.C., van Knippenberg, F.C., & Neijt, J.P. (1990). Measuring psychological and physical distress in cancer patients: structure and application of the Rotterdam Symptom Checklist. *British Journal of Cancer, 62*(6), 1034-1038.

Hagedoorn, M., Sanderman, R., Bolks, H.N., Tuinstra, J., & Coyne, J.C. (2008). Distress in couples coping with cancer: a meta-analysis and critical review of role and gender effects. *Psychological Bulletin, 134*(1), 1-30.

Hamer, M., Chida, Y., & Molloy, G.J. (2009). Psychological distress and cancer mortality. *Journal of Psychosomatic Research, 66,* 255-258.

Herschbach, P., Book, K., Brandl, T., Keller, M., Lindena, G., Neuwöhner, K., & Marten-Mittag, B. (2008). Psychological distress in cancer patients assessed with an expert rating scale. *British Journal of Cancer, 8*;99(1), 37-43.

Herschbach, P., Keller, M., Knight, L., Brandl, T., Huber, B., Henrich, G., & Marten-Mittag, B. (2004). Psychological problems of cancer patients: a cancer distress screening with a cancer-specific questionnaire. *British Journal of Cancer, 2*;91(3), 504-511.

Herschbach, P., Marten-Mittag, B., & Henrich, G. (2003). Revision und psychometrische Prüfung des Fragebogens zur Belastung von Krebskranken (FBK-R23). *Zeitschrift fuer Medizinische Psychologie, 12*(2), 1–8.

Hodges, L.J., Humphris, G.M., & Macfarlane, G. (2005). A metaanalytic investigation of the relationship between the psychological distress of cancer patients and their carers. *Social Science & Medicine, 60*, 1-12.

Holland, J.C. (1997). Preliminary guidelines for the treatment of distress. *Oncology, 11*, 109-114.

Holland, J.C., & Alici, Y. (2010). Management of distress in cancer patients. *Journal of Supportive Oncology, 8*, 4-12.

Iconomou, G., Iconomou, A.V., Argyriou, A.A., Nikolopoulos, A., Ifanti, A.A., & Kalofonos, H.P. (2008). Emotional distress in cancer patients at the beginning of chemotherapy and its relation to quality of life. *Journal of Balkan Union of Oncology, 13*(2), 217-222.

Jacobsen, P.B. (2009). Promoting evidence-based psychosocial care for cancer patients. *Psycho-Oncology, 18*, 6-13.

Jacobsen, P.B., Donovan, K.A., Zöe, N.S., & Watson, I.S. (2006). Management of anxiety and depression in adult cancer patients: toward an evidence-based approach. In A.E. Chang, P.A. Ganz, D.F. Hayes, et al. (Eds.), *Oncology: an evidence-based approach* (pp. 1561-1588). New York: Springer-Verlag.

Kadan-Lottick, N.S., Vanderwerker, L.C., Block, S.D., Zhang, B., & Prigerson, H.G. (2005). Psychiatric disorders and mental health service use in patients with advanced cancer: a report from the Coping with Cancer study. *Cancer, 104*, 2872-2881.

Keller, M., Sommerfeldt, S., Fischer, C., Knight, L., Riesbeck, M., Löwe, B., Herfarth, C., & Lehnert, T. (2004). Recognition of distress and psychiatric morbidity in cancer patients: a multi-method approach. *Annals of Oncology, 15*(8), 1243-1249.

Kelly, B., Smithers, M., Swanson, C., McLeod, R., Thomson, B., & Walpole, E. (1995). Psychological responses to malignant melanoma. An investigation of traumatic stress reactions to life-threatening illness. *General Hospital Psychiatry, 17*, 126-134.

Linden, W., Yi, D., Barroetavena, M., MacKenzie, R., & Doll, R. (2005). Development and validation of a psychosocial screening instrument for cancer. *Health Quality of Life Outcomes, 3*(1), 54.

Lloyd-Williams, M., Shiels, C., & Dowrick, C. (2007). The development of the Brief Edinburgh Depression Scale (BEDS) to screen for depression in patients with advanced cancer. *Journal of Affective Disorders, 99*(1–3), 259–264.

Luckett, T., Butow, P.N., King, M.T., Oguchi, M., Heading, G., Hackl, N.A., Rankin, N., & Price, M.A. (2010). A review and recommendations for optimal outcome measures of anxiety, depression and general distress in studies evaluating psychosocial interventions for English-speaking adults with heterogeneous cancer diagnoses. *Supportive Care in Cancer, 18*, 1241-1262.

Lueboonthavatchai, P. (2007). Prevalence and psychosocial factors of anxiety and depression in breast cancer patients. *Journal of The Medical Association of Thailand, 90*(10), 2164-2174.

Matthews, A.P. (2003). Role and gender differences in cancer-related distress: a comparison of survivor and caregiver self-reports. *Oncology Nursing Forum, 30*(3), 493-499.

Matthews, B.A., Baker, F., & Spillers, R.L. (2003). Family caregivers and indicators of cancer-related distress. *Psychology, Health, and Medicine, 8*, 45-56.

McLean, L.M., & Jones, J.M. (2007). A review of distress and its management in couples facing end-of-life cancer. *Psycho-Oncology, 16*(7), 603-617.

Mitchell, A.J. (2010). Short screening tools for cancer-related distress: a review and diagnostic validity meta-Analysis. *Journal of the National Comprehensive Cancer Network, 8*(4).

Moorey, S., & Greer, S. (1997). Adjuvant psychological therapy for cancer patients. *Palliative Medicine*;11(3), 240–244.

Morasso, G., Costantini, M., Baracco, G., Borreani, C., & Capelli, M. (1996). Assessing psychological distress in cancer patients: validation of a self-administered questionnaire. *Oncology, 53*(4), 295-302.

National Comprehensive Cancer Network (1999). Distress management. *Clinical practice guidelines, 1*, 344-374.

National Comprehensive Cancer Network (2003). Distress management clinical practice guidelines. *Journal of National Comprehensive Cancer Network, 1*, 344-374.

National Comprehensive Cancer Network (2011). Distress management. *Clinical practice guidelines in oncology, version 2011.*

Osborne, R.H., Elsworth, G.R., & Hopper, J.L. (2003). Age-specific norms and determinants of anxiety and depression in 731 women with breast cancer recruited through a population-based cancer registry. *European Journal of Cancer, 39*, 755-762.

Pasquini, M., Biondi, M., Costantini, A., Cairoli, F., Ferrarese, G., Picadi, A., & Sternberg, C. (2006). Detection and reatment of depressive and anxiety disorders among cancer patients: feasibility and preliminary findings from a liaison service in an oncology division. *Depression and Anxiety, 23*, 441-448.

Pirl, W.F. (2004). Evidence report on the occurence, assessment, and treatment of depression in cancer patients. *Journal of the National Cancer Institute Monograph*, 32-39.

Pitceathly, C., & Maguire, P. (2003). The psychological impact of cancer on patients' partners and other key relatives: a review. *European Journal of Cancer, 39*(11), 1517-1524.

Rabin, C., Rogers, M.L., Pinto, B.M., Nash, J.M., Frierson, G.M., & Trask, P.C. (2007). Effect of personal cancer history and family cancer history on levels of psychological distress. *Social Science & Medicine, 64*, 411–416.

Radloff, L.S. (1977). The CES-D scale: a self-report depression scale for research in the general population. *Applied Psychological Measurement, 1*(3), 385-401.

Ryan, H., Schofield, P., Cockburn, J., Butow, P., Tattersall, M., Turner, J., Girgis, A., Bandaranayake, D., & Bowman, D. (2005). How to recognize and manage psychological distress in cancer patients. *European Journal of Cancer Care, 14*, 7-15.

Sellick, S.M., & Edwardson, A.D. (2007). Screening new cancer patients for psychological distress using the Hospital Anxiety and Depression Scale. *Psycho-Oncology, 16*, 534-542.

Simonelli, C., Annunziata, M.A., Chimienti, E., Berretta, M., & Tirelli, U. (2008). Cancer survivorship: a challenge for the European oncologists. *Annals of Oncology, 19*(7), 1216-1217.

Simonelli, C., Berretta, M., Tirelli, U., & Annunziata, M.A. (2008). Clinical management of long-term cancer survivors. *Journal of Clinical Oncology, 26*(1), 161-162.

Società Italiana di Psico-Oncologia - SIPO (1998). Standard, opzioni e raccomandazioni per una buona pratica psico-oncologica. www.siponazionale.it

Stark, D., & Housel, A. (2000). Anxiety in cancer patients. *British Journal of Cancer, 83*, 1261-1267.

Stark, D., Kiely, M., Smith, A., Velikova, G., House, A.,& Selby, P. (2002). Anxiety disorders in cancer patients: their nature, associations, and relation to quality of life. *Journal of Clinical Oncology, 20*, 3137-3148.

Strong, V., Waters, R., Hibberd, C., Rush, R., Cargill, A., Storey, D., Walker, J., Wall, L., Fallon, M., & Sharpe, M. (2007). Emotional distress in cancer patients: the Edinburgh Cancer Centre symptom study. *British Journal of Cancer, 26*;96(6), 868-874.

van't Spijker, A., Trijsburg, R.W., & Duivenvoorden, H.J. (1997). Psychological sequelae of cancer diagnosis: a meta-analytical review of 58 studies after 1980. *Psychosomatic Medicine, 59*, 280-293.

Vodermaier, A., Linden, W., & Siu, C. (2009). Screening for emotional distress in cancer patients: a systematic review of assessment instruments. *Journal of National Cancer Institute, 101*, 1464-1488.

Weihs, K., & Reiss, D. (1996). Family reorganization in response to cancer: a development perspective. In L. Baider, C.L. Cooper, D.E. Kaplan, A. Nour (Eds.), *Cancer and the family* (pp. 17-39). New York: John Wiley & Sons, Ltd.

Williams, S., & Dale, J. (2006). The effectiveness of treatment for depression/depressive symptoms in adult with cancer: a systematic review. *British Journal of Cancer, 94*, 372-390.

Zabora, J.R. (1998). Screening procedures for psychosocial distress. In J.C. Holland, W. Breibart, P.B. Jacobsen, et al. (Eds.), *Psycho-Oncology* (pp. 653-661). New York: Oxford University Press.

Zabora, J., Binzzenhofeszoc, K., Burbow, B., Hooker, C., & Piantadosi, S. (2001). The prevalence of psychological distress by cancer site. *Psycho-Oncology, 10*, 19-28.

Zigmond, A.S., & Snaith, R.P. (1983). The Hospital Anxiety and Depression Scale. *Acta Psychiatrica Scandinavica, 67*(6), 361–370.

Zwahlen, D., Hagenbuch, N., Carley, M.I., Recklitis, C.J., & Buchi, S. (2008). Screening cancer patients' families with the distress thermometer (DT): a validation study. *Psycho-Oncology, 17*, 959-966.

In: Psychological Distress   ISBN: 978-1-61942-646-7
Editors: H. Ohayashi and S. Yamada   © 2012 Nova Science Publishers, Inc.

Chapter 3

SCREENING FOR PSYCHOLOGICAL DISTRESS

Pekka Johannes Puustinen
Centre for Social and Health Services, Kuopio, Finland;
School of Medicine, Unit of Primary Health Care,
University of Eastern Finland, Kuopio, Finland

ABSTRACT

Psychological distress is a term used to describe the general psychopathology of an individual - a combination of depressive symptoms, anxiety and perceived stress. The term poses a wider perspective to psychopathology compared to clinically diagnosed diseases, including also symptoms falling below the diagnostic threshold for a given disorder. Thus, especially in community and primary care settings screening tools for measuring also subthreshold psychological disorders and general psychological distress may aid early detection and timely intervention for people at risk.

The 12-item General Health Questionnaire (GHQ-12), introduced by David Goldberg in 1972, is one of the most widely used and studied indicators of psychological distress. The prevalence of high psychological distress measured by the GHQ-12 varies from 15% to 36% across different studies, countries and by the cut-off points used. The GHQ-12 is associated with various sociodemographic and behavioural variables, which must be taken into account when screening for psychological distress in the population level. Screening for psychological distress in clinical practice is improved, when targeted carefully.

INTRODUCTION

McGraw-Hill Concise Dictionary of Modern Medicine (2002) defines psychological distress as "the end result of factors– e.g., psychogenic pain, internal conflicts, and external stress that prevent a person from self-actualization and connecting with 'significant others'" [1]. Although there is no universally accepted definition for psychological distress, most definitions widen the range of psychopathology from clinically diagnosed diseases (e.g. depression or anxiety disorders) to symptoms falling below the diagnostic threshold for a given disorder. This is relevant for number of reasons. First, subthreshold psychological disorders are common. In a study of 554 primary care patients by Rucci et al. [2], the prevalence of subthreshold depressive and anxiety disorders was 9.9% and 8.3%, respectively – both exceeding the prevalence of corresponding clinical disorders (4.6% and 7.6%, respectively). Olfson et al. [3] reported that subthreshold symptoms were more common than their respective clinical diagnoses in a sample of 1001 adult primary care patients: panic (10.5% vs. 4.8%), depression (9.1% vs. 7.3%), anxiety (6.6% vs. 3.7%) and obsessive-compulsive (5.8% vs. 1.4%).

Second, even subthreshold level symptoms are associated with reduced quality of life and functional impairment. Collings et al. [4] found that in a sample of 775 primary care patients there was no significant difference in the level of disability between patients with subthreshold disorders and patients with clinical disorders. In a large WHO Collaborative Study on psychological problems in general health care, covering 14 countries, most major cultures and languages and over 25 000 patients, a dose-response relationship was found between severity of mental illness and disability [5]. Also Berardi et al. [6] reported similar results in their sample of 323 primary care attenders: the prevalence of clinical disorders and subthreshold disorders was 12.4% and 18% respectively and significant impairment in physical and mental functioning was seen in both categories.

Third, there is an elevated risk for individuals with subthreshold disorders for developing full-syndromal psychiatric disorder [7]. In a study by Lewinsohn et al. [8] with 3003 subjects from all age groups from adolescents to elderly, increasing levels of depressive symptoms were associated with elevated incidence of major depression and increasing levels of psychosocial dysfunction.

This suggests that depression and other psychological disorders may best be conceptualized as a continuum and especially in community and primary care settings screening tools for measuring also subthreshold psychological disorders and general psychological distress may aid early detection and timely intervention for people at risk [9].

SCREENING TOOLS: THE 12-ITEM GENERAL HEALTH QUESTIONNAIRE

Psychiatric researchers have developed and used a bewildering variety of assessment tools to detect psychopathology among patients and in the community level. The Symptom Checklist 90 (SCL-90) [10], Hamilton Rating Scale for Depression (HRSD) [11,12], Montgomery-Åsberg Depression Rating Scale (MADRS) [13], Kessler Psychological Distress Scale (K10 and K6) [14], Beck Depression Inventory (BDI) [15], the Revised Clinical Interview Scale (CIS-R) [16] and the Everyday Feeling Questionnaire (EFQ) [17] are among the best validated assessment instruments.

The General Health Questionnaire (GHQ) [18,19], introduced by David Goldberg in 1972, is one of the most widely used and studied indicators of psychological distress. It is also in many ways ideal for screening purposes. In fact, some studies have referred the GHQ as "the current de facto standard of mental health screening" [20]. The original GHQ had 60, 36, 30 or 12 items (GHQ-60, GHQ-36, GHQ-30 and GHQ-12), but already in 1979 Goldberg and Hillier introduced a scaled version of the GHQ, based on 28 items derived from a factor analysis of the 60-items scale (GHQ-28) [21]. GHQ-28 contained four subscales: somatic symptoms, anxiety and insomnia, social dysfunction and severe depression.

The shortest version (GHQ-12) is contained within in 30, 36 and 60-item questionnaire, but it contains no questions about somatic symptoms [19]. It has gained acceptance as a screening tool, because of its space-saving properties in survey studies. GHQ-12 is comprised of twelve questions regarding general level of happiness, experience of depressive and anxiety symptoms, perceived stress and sleep disturbance over the last four weeks (Table 1). Six of the questions are positively phrased (questions 1,3,4,7,8 and 12) and six negatively phrased.

Each question has a four-point response scale: for positively phrased questions e.g. feeling reasonable happy (better than usual, same as usual, worse than usual, much worse than usual) and for negatively phrased questions e.g. feeling unhappy and depressed (not at all, no more than usual, more than usual, much more than usual).

Table. 1. The 12-item General Health Questionnaire items

Have you recently:

1. Been able to concentrate on whatever you are doing?
2. Lost much sleep over worry?
3. Felt that you are playing a useful part in things?
4. Felt capable of making decisions about things?
5. Felt constantly under strain?
6. Felt you could not overcome your difficulties?
7. Been able to enjoy your normal day-to-day activities?
8. Been able to face up to your problems?
9. Been feeling unhappy and depressed?
10. Been losing confidence in yourself?
11. Been thinking yourself as a worthless person?
12. Been feeling reasonably happy all things concerned

The original rating method of the four-point response scale is referred as the GHQ (or binary) method (0-0-1-1; e.g. for negatively phrased questions: not at all = 0, no more than usual = 0, more than usual = 1, much more than usual = 1) [19] and the points are summed to a global score ranging from 0-12. Another way of rating the questionnaire is the so-called modified Likert scoring method, in which the overall score is calculated by assigning separate scores (0-3) to each response and summing across the items [22]. Goodshild and Duncan-Jones [23] proposed yet another scoring method (C-GHQ method), where the positively phrased items are coded 0-0-1-1 and the negatively phrased 0-1-1-1. They argue that the response "no more than usual", to a negatively phrased item describing pathology, should be treated as an indicator of chronic illness rather that of good health. Although all the scoring methods have been used in the past, most research using the GHQ-12 during the last decade has relied on the GHQ method.

There are many validating studies of the GHQ-12 in different countries, cultures and languages. In the WHO study of mental illness in general health care, Goldberg et al. [24] have validated the GHQ-12 against standardized psychiatric interviews for 5438 patients across 15 centers around the world. The results were uniformly good, with the average area under the ROC curve 0.88, range from 0.83 to 0.95. Additionally, complex scoring methods (C-GHQ and Likert methods) offered no advantages over the simpler GHQ method.

There may be significant variations in the best threshold values of the GHQ-12 in detecting psychiatric morbidity in different countries and cultures. In the above-mentioned WHO study by Goldberg et al. [24], the optimal thresholds varied across the 15 study centers: 1/2 (8 centers), 2/3 (5 centers), 3/4 (one center) and 6/7 (one center).

The reported prevalence figures for high psychological distress measured by the GHQ-12 vary from 15% to 36% across different studies, countries and by the cut-off points used. In a population-based sample of 4501 adults in North-West of England, 28% of the subjects scored 4-12 points indicating high psychological distress [25]. Harrison et al. [26] reported similar prevalence (27% for high psychological distress) in an English study of 38000 responders. In the Scottish Health Survey with 6576 healthy men and women, 959 subjects (15%) were categorized as high distressed [27]. In a Nigerian sample of 272 primary care patients, 21% was categorized as psychologically distressed [28]. Furthermore, in study of 4867 primary health care patients in Australia, 36% had scores on GHQ-12 indicating psychological distress [29]. In the Health 2000 Study in Finland with a representative population sample of 8028 subjects, the mean GHQ-12 score for men was 1.68 and for women 1.95 [30].

In most studies, the GHQ-12 has been used as a unidimensional measure. There are factor analysis studies, however, which challenge this view. In 1991, Graetz [31] introduced a three-factor model arguing that GHQ-12 measures psychiatric dysfunction in three domains (social dysfunction, anxiety and loss of confidence). The three factor model has gained support also in other studies [32-40], while other studies have identified only two factors, most commonly named depression and social dysfunction [38,41-45].

However, none of the complete factor models that have been proposed have been consistently replicated across studies [46]. Furthermore, using the proposed factors separately does not seem to offer many practical advantages in differentiating clinical groups or identifying association with clinical or health-related quality of life variables [33]. It has also been argued that the division of the GHQ-12 into positively phrased and negatively phrased statements could introduce response bias, which should be taken into account when deriving factors [47]. When this possible bias was taken into account, superiority of the unidimensional model has been reported [48].

There has been some debate about the conceptual overlap between psychological distress and other, clinically distinct psychiatric disorders, e.g. depression and anxiety. Thus, the rationale of screening general psychological distress with GHQ-12 instead of measuring, for instance, the level of depression with distinct assessment tool can be questioned. However, the results of some factor analyses studies suggest, that comorbidity between different psychiatric disorders results from common, underlying core psychopathological processes [49,50] and the authors of these studies suggest that the research should be focused on these core processes themselves, rather than on their varied manifestations as separate disorders.

Hotopf et al. [51] studied the relationship between four psychiatric assessment tools within a mixed primary care population. The assessment tools in the study included Hamilton Rating Scale for Depression (HRSD), Beck Depression Inventory (BDI), the Revised Clinical Interview Scale (CIS-R) and the 12-item General Health Questionnaire. Despite of the similarities, the different screening instruments are not identical. First, the instruments were originally designed for different uses: the GHQ-12 is a screening instrument for psychiatric disorders in the community, whereas the BDI and HRSD are supposed to be used in patients with previously diagnosed depression and to monitor the severity of depression. The CIS-R is meant to be used as a diagnostic interview capable of detecting ten diagnoses, but it also produces a global score of severity. Second, GHQ-12 and BDI are self-administered questionnaires, the HRSD is based on an unstructured clinical interview and the CIS-R is a structured interview. Third, although there is considerable conceptual overlap between the instruments (from 32 different symptoms that contribute to the global score of the BDI, HRSD and CIS-R, only 9 are unique to any other scale [51]), the GHQ-12 also measures anxiety and perceived stress in addition to depressive symptoms.

According to Hotopf et al. [51], the total score for each of the four scales correlated closely with every other one (correlation coefficients = 0.70 – 0.79). Lipsanen et al. [52] reported similar, high correlations between GHQ-12, BDI and the somatization part of the Symptom Check List 90 (SCL-90) (correlation coefficients = 0.68 and 0.46, respectively). They concluded that while psychological distress, depression and somatization are distinct constructs, they correlate to a considerable extend.

Although GHQ-12 has wide acceptance as a screening instrument, there is debate about the efficacy of screening and case detection for psychological factors in clinical practice. When compared to normal circumstances without screening, GHQ-12 used in an ordinary general practice environment was able to detect one additional patient with a real diagnostic psychological problem for every five patients screened, when used with infrequently seen patients, but screening of well-known patients provided less additional cases [53]. This implicates that the effectiveness of screening for psychological distress in clinical practice is improved, when carefully targeted.

ASSOCIATIONS OF GHQ-12 WITH SOCIODEMOGRAPHIC AND BEHAVIOURAL VARIABLES

The GHQ-12 is associated with various sociodemographic and behavioural variables. These associations are summed in Table 2. It is of utmost importance to take these associations into account when screening for psychological distress in the population level.

It has been long known that women generally report higher levels of depression, psychiatric disorders and distress compared to men [54,55]. Similar association has been observed also in the studies using the GHQ-12. In the North West Regional Health Needs Survey with 38 000 responders, 29% of women scored above the GHQ threshold of 3, compared to 23% of men [26]. In the Scottish Health Survey of 6576 healthy men and women, risk for high psychological distress (GHQ-12 points 4 or more) was higher among women compared to men (OR 1.61 after adjusting with age, health behaviours and obesity) [27].

In the British Whitehall II study (n=3116) and in the Finnish Helsinki Health Study (n=6028), the age-adjusted prevalence of high psychological distress (GHQ-12 points 3 or more) was higher among women in both studies (26% vs. 23% in Helsinki, 29% vs. 23% in London) [56]. In another Finnish study (The Health 2000 Study) by Pirkola et al. [30] with a nationally representative sample of 8028 subjects, the mean GHQ-12 score for men was 1.68 and for women 1.95. Thus, there seems to be a clear gender difference in psychological distress, which possibly cannot be explained with other confounding factors: Weich et al. [57] reported in their longitudinal study of 9947 subjects using the data from the British Household Panel Survey that this gender difference in psychological distress was not explained by type of social roles occupied nor socio-economic status.

The relationship between age and psychological distress measured by the GHQ-12 is controversial. In the population-based study by Hamer et al. [58] with 15158 subjects, age was not statistically related to psychological distress. Robinson et al. [25] reported similar, nonsignificant, results in a population-based study in North West England. However, in the Finnish Health 2000 Study, the age of 65 or more was significantly associated with high psychological distress after adjusting with gender and physical health [30].

Table 2. Associations of GHQ-12 with sociodemographic and behavioural variables according to literature

	High psychological distress (GHQ-12)				
	Strong support for positive association	Some support for positive association	No clear association	Some support for negative association	Strong support for negative association
Female gender	+				
Higher age		+			
High education				+	
Living alone	+				
Smoking	+				
Regular physical activity					+
Regular alcohol consumption		+			
Obesity		+			

Faris and Dunham [59] demonstrated already in 1939 an inverse relationship between socio-economic status and mental disorders. In their review of five large-scale population-based studies in 2003, Fryers et al. [60] found a positive association between less education and high psychological distress in four out of five studies. Since then, population based studies using the GHQ-12 have yielded mixed results. In the study of 5703 women in rural India, higher education was less often associated with high psychological distress (GHQ-12 points 5 or more) compared to low education (OR 0.6) [61]. Belek [62] reported similar, significant association in his study of 1092 adults in Turkey. However, in the study of 6028 Finnish and 3116 English public sector employees, no association was found between education level and high psychological distress measured by GHQ-12 points of 3 or more [56]. Thus, the relationship between education and psychological distress is yet to be fully elucidated.

Marital status has been associated with psychological distress measured by the GHQ-12 in previously published studies. Using the population-based data from the Scottish Health Survey with 13158 study subjects, Hamer et al. [58] reported that psychologically distressed subjects (GHQ-12 points 4 or more) were significantly less often married than non-distressed subjects (51%

vs. 65%). Similar statistically significant association was also reported in a Chinese study with 14632 subjects [63]. In a Finnish study among 3949 white-collar workers, living with spouse/partner decreased significantly the odds for high psychological distress for women (OR 0.77), among men there was no significant association [64].

It is generally known that adverse health behaviors may arise as a coping response to psychological distress. Adler and Mathews [65] conducted an extensive review of literature in this field in 1994. They concluded that psychological distress is indeed associated with health-damaging behaviors, such as smoking, sedentary lifestyle and excessive use of alcohol. Since then numerous studies have focused on these associations.

High levels of psychological distress are associated with higher levels of smoking [66-69], although some studies suggest that among different ethnic groups, this association is relatively specific to white individuals [70]. This association between psychological distress and smoking has been observed also among studies using GHQ-12. In their population-based study of 4501 subjects, Robinson et al. [25] found that subjects with high psychological distress (GHQ-12 points 4 or more) were much more likely to smoke compared to subjects with no psychological distress (20% vs. 6%). Hamer et al. [27] reported similar, although higher prevalences from the Scottish Health Survey (43% vs. 27%). Among Finnish white-collar employees, current smokers were more likely to have GHQ-12 points 3 or more indicating psychological distress (OR for women: 1.29, OR for men: 1.70) [64].

In the U.S. National Comorbidity Survey with 8093 adult subjects, a negative association was found between regular physical activity and depressive and anxiety disorders [71]. Also in the nationwide Norwegian survey with 12310 subjects in the age of 30-60 years, exercise was negatively associated with psychological distress (OR 0.76) [72]. Ezoe et al. [73] found that after controlling for age, marital status and somatic conditions, physical exercise was significantly related to psychological distress measured by the GHQ-28 in the sample of 2800 male and female Japanese factory workers. Hamer et al. [74] used the GHQ-12 in the Scottish Health Survey with 19842 healthy men and women. Any form of daily physical activity was associated with a lower risk of psychological distress (based on a score of 4 or more on the GHQ-12) after adjustment for age, gender, social economic group, marital status, body mass index, long-standing illness, smoking and survey year (OR 0.59). A dose-response relationship was apparent, with moderate reductions in psychological distress with less frequent activity. Among Finnish white-collar employees (n=3949), physically inactive subjects were more likely to have

GHQ-12 points 3 or more indicating psychological distress (OR for women: 1.21, OR for men: 1.81) [64].

The association between high psychological distress measured by the GHQ-12 and alcohol consumption is controversial. In a study among Royal Navy personnel with a sample of 2236 subject, high psychological distress (GHQ-12 score 4 or more) was a risk factor for heavy drinking (22-42 units of alcohol per week) but not for binge drinking (drinking 9 or more units in a drinking session) [75]. Also Hamer et al. [27] reported that the mean alcohol consumption (units/week) among psychologically distressed subjects was significantly higher compared to non-distressed subjects (21 vs. 17 for men, 8 vs. 6 for women). However, in a study among medical students in Chile, no association was observed between psychological distress and alcohol consumption [76]. Also the two Finnish studies by Saarni et al. [77] and Laaksonen et al. [64] yielded no significant association between alcohol consumption and psychological distress.

There has been some support for the association between obesity and psychological distress. McElroy et al. [78] conducted an extensive review of the literature in 2004 and concluded that there is an association between psychological distress and obesity, particularly in women. Among men, the results were inconclusive. In the Scottish Health Survey with 6576 healthy men and women, 20.8% of non-distressed subjects (GHQ-12 points 0-3) and 22.8% of distressed subjects (GHQ-12 $\geq$ 4) were reported obese (BMI > 30) [27]. However, when adjusting with age, gender and health behaviours, this association was no longer significant. Among university employees in Rio de Janeiro, BMI showed a significant association with psychological distress in women, but not in men [79]. After adjusting with income and self-reported health problems, also this association did not persist. Other series of studies have explored the opposite causal direction—that is, obesity as a risk factor for future mental disorder. Again, the results from these studies have been contradictory [80]. However, in a literature review by Atlantis et al. [81], a weak level of evidence was observed supporting the hypothesis that obesity increases the incidence of mental disorders.

Several mechanisms could explain these two causal directions. In societies in which obesity is stigmatized, this may lead to increased risk of psychological distress [82]. On the other hand, psychological distress is associated with disordered eating, which could lead to obesity in the future [83]. Kivimäki et al. [80] studied the direction of association between psychological distress measured by the GHQ-30 and obesity among 4363 adults in prospective cohort study with four measurements over 19 years. They concluded that the direction of causality is from psychological distress to increased future risk of obesity. This association was also cumulative with repeated episodes of psychological distress.

CONCLUSION

In conclusion, based on the literature review, GHQ-12 can be seen as a recommended screening tool for psychological distress for number of reasons. First, the GHQ-12 was originally designed to be used as a screening instrument in the community level. Second, it is a self-administrated questionnaire, which can be filled quickly. Third, it is one of the most widely studied indicators of psychological distress and fourth, it has been validated in numerous studies across different countries, cultures and languages. However, the GHQ-12 is associated with various sociodemographic and behavioural variables, which must be taken into account when screening for psychological distress in the population level.

REFERENCES

[1]   Segen JC editor. Concise Dictionary of Modern Medicine. USA: The McGraw-Hill Companies, Inc.; 2002.

[2]   Rucci P, Gherardi S, Tansella M, Piccinelli M, Berardi D, Bisoffi G, et al. Subthreshold psychiatric disorders in primary care: prevalence and associated characteristics. *J. Affect. Disord.* 2003 Sep;76(1-3):171-181.

[3]   Olfson M, Broadhead WE, Weissman MM, Leon AC, Farber L, Hoven C, et al. Subthreshold psychiatric symptoms in a primary care group practice. *Arch. Gen. Psychiatry.* 1996 Oct;53(10):880-886.

[4]   Collings S, MaGPIe Research Group. Disability and the detection of mental disorder in primary care. *Soc. Psychiatry. Psychiatr. Epidemiol.* 2005 Dec;40(12):994-1002.

[5]   Ormel J, VonKorff M, Ustun TB, Pini S, Korten A, Oldehinkel T. Common mental disorders and disability across cultures. Results from the WHO Collaborative Study on Psychological Problems in General Health Care. *JAMA* 1994 Dec 14;272(22):1741-1748.

[6]   Berardi D, Berti Ceroni G, Leggieri G, Rucci P, Ustun B, Ferrari G. Mental, physical and functional status in primary care attenders. *Int. J. Psychiatry. Med.* 1999;29(2):133-148.

[7]   Cuijpers P, Smit F, Willemse G. Predicting the onset of major depression in subjects with subthreshold depression in primary care: a prospective study. *Acta. Psychiatr. Scand.* 2005 Feb;111(2):133-138.

[8]   Lewinsohn PM, Solomon A, Seeley JR, Zeiss A. Clinical implications of "subthreshold" depressive symptoms. *J. Abnorm. Psychol.* 2000 May;109(2):345-351.

[9]   Karsten J, Nolen WA, Penninx BW, Hartman CA. Subthreshold anxiety better defined by symptom self-report than by diagnostic interview. *J. Affect. Disord.* 2010 Oct 16.

[10] Derogatis LR, Lipman RS, Covi L. SCL-90: an outpatient psychiatric rating scale--preliminary report. *Psychopharmacol Bul.l* 1973 Jan;9(1):13-28.

[11] Hamilton M. A rating scale for depression. *J. Neurol. Neurosurg. Psychiatry.* 1960 Feb;23:56-62.

[12] Hamilton M. Rating depressive patients. *J. Clin. Psychiatry.* 1980 Dec;41(12 Pt 2):21-24.

[13] Montgomery SA, Asberg M. A new depression scale designed to be sensitive to change. *Br. J. Psychiatry.* 1979 Apr;134:382-389.

[14] Kessler RC, Andrews G, Colpe LJ, Hiripi E, Mroczek DK, Normand SL, et al. Short screening scales to monitor population prevalences and trends in non-specific psychological distress. *Psychol. Med.* 2002 Aug;32(6):959-976.

[15] Beck AT, Ward CH, Mendelson M, Mock J, Erbaugh J. An inventory for measuring depression. *Arch. Gen. Psychiatry.* 1961 Jun;4:561-571.

[16] Lewis G, Pelosi AJ, Araya R, Dunn G. Measuring psychiatric disorder in the community: a standardized assessment for use by lay interviewers. *Psychol. Med.* 1992 May;22(2):465-486.

[17] Uher R, Goodman R. The Everyday Feeling Questionnaire: the structure and validation of a measure of general psychological well-being and distress. *Soc. Psychiatry. Psychiatr. Epidemiol.* 2010 Mar;45(3):413-423.

[18] Goldberg DP editor. The detection of psychiatric illness by questionnaire. Maudsley monograph no. 21. London: Oxford University Press; 1972.

[19] Goldberg DP, Williams P editors. A User's Guide to the General Health Questionnaire. Windsor, United Kingdom: NFER - Nelson; 1988.

[20] Furukawa TA, Kessler RC, Slade T, Andrews G. The performance of the K6 and K10 screening scales for psychological distress in the Australian National Survey of Mental Health and Well-Being. *Psychol. Med.* 2003 Feb;33(2):357-362.

[21] Goldberg DP, Hillier VF. A scaled version of the General Health Questionnaire. *Psychol. Med.* 1979 Feb;9(1):139-145.

[22] Banks MH, Clegg CW, Jackson PR, Kemp NJ, Stafford EM, Wall TD. The use of the General Health Questionnaire as an indicator of mental health in occupational studies. *J. Occup. Psychology.* 1980;53:187-194.

[23] Goodchild ME, Duncan-Jones P. Chronicity and the General Health Questionnaire. *Br. J. Psychiatry.* 1985 Jan;146:55-61.

[24] Goldberg DP, Gater R, Sartorius N, Ustun TB, Piccinelli M, Gureje O, et al. The validity of two versions of the GHQ in the WHO study of mental illness in general health care. Psychol Med 1997 Jan;27(1):191-197.

[25] Robinson KL, McBeth J, Macfarlane GJ. Psychological distress and premature mortality in the general population: a prospective study. *Ann. Epidemiol.* 2004 Aug;14(7):467-472.

[26] Harrison J, Barrow S, Creed F. Mental health in the north west region of England: associations with deprivation. *Soc. Psychiatry. Psychiatr. Epidemiol.* 1998 Mar;33(3):124-128.

[27] Hamer M, Molloy GJ, Stamatakis E. Psychological distress as a risk factor for cardiovascular events: pathophysiological and behavioral mechanisms. *J. Am. Coll. Cardiol.* 2008 Dec 16;52(25):2156-2162.

[28] Abiodun OA. A study of mental morbidity among primary care patients in Nigeria. *Compr. Psychiatry.* 1993 Jan-Feb;34(1):10-13.

[29] Harris MF, Silove D, Kehag E, Barratt A, Manicavasagar V, Pan J, et al. Anxiety and depression in general practice patients: prevalence and management. *Med. J. Aust.* 1996 May 6;164(9):526-529.

[30] Pirkola S, Saarni S, Suvisaari J, Elovainio M, Partonen T, Aalto AM, et al. General health and quality-of-life measures in active, recent, and comorbid mental disorders: a population-based health 2000 study. *Compr. Psychiatry.* 2009 Mar-Apr;50(2):108-114.

[31] Graetz B. Multidimensional properties of the General Health Questionnaire. *Soc. Psychiatry. Psychiatr. Epidemiol.* 1991;26(3):132-138.

[32] Cheung YB. A confirmatory factor analysis of the 12-item General Health Questionnaire among older people. *Int. J. Geriatr. Psychiatry.* 2002 Aug;17(8):739-744.

[33] Gao F, Luo N, Thumboo J, Fones C, Li S, Cheung Y,. Does the 12-item General Health Questionnaire contain multiple factors and do we need them? 2004.

[34] Ip WY, Martin CR. Factor structure of the Chinese version of the 12-item General Health Questionnaire (GHQ-12) in pregnancy. *J. Repr. Inf. Psychol.* 2006;24(2):87-98.

[35] Makikangas A, Feldt T, Kinnunen U, Tolvanen A, Kinnunen ML, Pulkkinen L. The factor structure and factorial invariance of the 12-item General Health Questionnaire (GHQ-12) across time: evidence from two community-based samples. *Psychol. Assess.* 2006 Dec;18(4):444-451.

[36] Martin CR, Newell RJ. The factor structure of the 12-item General Health Questionnaire in individuals with facial disfigurement. *J. Psychosom. Res.* 2005 Oct;59(4):193-199.

[37] Penninkilampi-Kerola V, Miettunen J, Ebeling H. A comparative assessment of the factor structures and psychometric properties of the GHQ-12 and the GHQ-20 based on data from a Finnish population-based sample. *Scand. J. Psychol.* 2006 Oct;47(5):431-440.

[38] Picardi A, Abeni D, Pasquini P. Assessing psychological distress in patients with skin diseases: reliability, validity and factor structure of the GHQ-12. *J. Eur. Acad. Dermatol. Venereol.* 2001 Sep;15(5):410-417.

[39] Sanchez-Lopez MP, Dresch V. The 12-Item General Health Questionnaire (GHQ-12): Reliability, external validity and factor structure in the Spanish population. *Psicothema* 2008 Nov;20(4):839-843.

[40] Shevlin M, Adamson G. Alternative factor models and factorial invariance of the GHQ-12: a large sample analysis using confirmatory factor analysis. *Psychol. Assess* .2005 Jun;17(2):231-236.

[41] Doi Y, Minowa M. Factor structure of the 12-item General Health Questionnaire in the Japanese general adult population. *Psychiatry. Clin. Neurosci.* 2003 Aug;57(4):379-383.

[42] Hu Y, Stewart-Brown S, Twigg L, Weich S. Can the 12-item General Health Questionnaire be used to measure positive mental health? *Psychol. Med.* 2007 Jul;37(7):1005-1013.

[43] Kalliath TJ, O'Driscoll MP, Brough P. A confirmatory factor analysis of the General Health Questionnaire - 12. Stress and Health: *Journal of the International Society for the Investigation of Stress* 2004;20(1):11-20.

[44] Vanheule S, Bogaerts S. Short Communication: The factorial structure of the GHQ-12. Stress and Health: *Journal of the International Society for the Investigation of Stress* 2005;21(4):217-222.

[45] Werneke U, Goldberg DP, Yalcin I, Ustun BT. The stability of the factor structure of the General Health Questionnaire. *Psychol. Med.* 2000 Jul;30(4):823-829.

[46] Campbell A, Walker J, Farrell G. Confirmatory factor analysis of the GHQ-12: can I see that again? *Aust. N. Z. J. Psychiatry.* 2003 Aug;37(4):475-483.

[47] Hankins M. The factor structure of the twelve item General Health Questionnaire (GHQ-12): the result of negative phrasing? *Clin. Pract. Epidemiol. Ment. Health.* 2008 Apr 24;4:10.

[48] Hankins M. The reliability of the twelve-item general health questionnaire (GHQ-12) under realistic assumptions. *BMC Public Health* 2008;8:355.

[49] Krueger RF. The structure of common mental disorders. *Arch. Gen. Psychiatry.* 1999 Oct;56(10):921-926.

[50] Vollebergh WA, Iedema J, Bijl RV, de Graaf R, Smit F, Ormel J. The structure and stability of common mental disorders: the NEMESIS study. *Arch. Gen. Psychiatry.* 2001 Jun;58(6):597-603.

[51] Hotopf M, Sharp D, Lewis G. What's in a name? A comparison of four psychiatric assessments. *Soc. Psychiatry. Psychiatr. Epidemiol.* 1998 Jan;33(1):27-31.

[52] Lipsanen T, Saarijarvi S, Lauerma H. Exploring the relations between depression, somatization, dissociation and alexithymia--overlapping or independent constructs? Psychopathology 2004 Jul-Aug;37(4):200-206.

[53] MaGPIe Research Group. The effectiveness of case-finding for mental health problems in primary care. *Br. J. Gen. Pract.* 2005 Sep;55 (518):665-669.

[54] Baum A, Grunberg NE. Gender, stress, and health. *Health Psychol.* 1991;10(2):80-85.

[55] McDonough P, Walters V. Gender and health: reassessing patterns and explanations. *Soc. Sci. Med.* 2001 Feb;52(4):547-559.

[56] Laaksonen E, Martikainen P, Lahelma E, Lallukka T, Rahkonen O, Head J, et al. Socioeconomic circumstances and common mental disorders among Finnish and British public sector employees: evidence from the Helsinki Health Study and the Whitehall II Study. *Int. J. Epidemiol.* 2007 Aug;36(4):776-786.

[57] Weich S, Sloggett A, Lewis G. Social roles and the gender difference in rates of the common mental disorders in Britain: a 7-year, population-based cohort study. *Psychol. Med.* 2001 Aug;31(6):1055-1064.

[58] Hamer M, Chida Y, Molloy GJ. Psychological distress and cancer mortality. *J. Psychosom. Res.* 2009 Mar;66(3):255-258.

[59] Faris RE, Dunham WW editors. Mental disoreders in urban areas. Chicago: University of Chicago Press; 1939.

[60] Fryers T, Melzer D, Jenkins R. Social inequalities and the common mental disorders: a systematic review of the evidence. *Soc. Psychiatry. Psychiatr. Epidemiol.* 2003 May;38(5):229-237.

[61] Shidhaye R, Patel V. Association of socio-economic, gender and health factors with common mental disorders in women: a population-based study of 5703 married rural women in India. *Int. J. Epidemiol.* 2010 Dec;39(6):1510-1521.

[62] Belek I. Social class, income, education, area of residence and psychological distress: does social class have an independent effect on psychological distress in Antalya, Turkey? *Soc. Psychiatry. Psychiatr. Epidemiol.* 2000 Feb;35(2):94-101.

[63] Gu YM, Xu FZ, Shi QC, Yang TZ, Li L. A multilevel cross-sectional study of mental disorder in community settings in Zhejiang Province]. *Zhonghua Yu Fang Yi Xue Za Zhi* 2009 Dec;43(12):1105-1108.

[64] Laaksonen E, Martikainen P, Lallukka T, Lahelma E, Ferrie J, Rahkonen O, et al. Economic difficulties and common mental disorders among Finnish and British white-collar employees: the contribution of social and behavioural factors. *J. Epidemiol. Community Health* 2009 Jun;63(6):439-446.

[65] Adler N, Matthews K. Health psychology: why do some people get sick and some stay well? *Annu. Rev. Psychol.* 1994;45:229-259.

[66] Kassel JD, Stroud LR, Paronis CA. Smoking, stress, and negative affect: correlation, causation, and context across stages of smoking. *Psychol. Bull.* 2003 Mar;129(2):270-304.

[67] Hagman BT, Delnevo CD, Hrywna M, Williams JM. Tobacco use among those with serious psychological distress: results from the national survey of drug use and health, 2002. *Addict. Behav.* 2008 Apr;33(4):582-592.

[68] Chaiton MO, Cohen JE, O'Loughlin J, Rehm J. A systematic review of longitudinal studies on the association between depression and smoking in adolescents. *BMC Public Health* 2009 Sep 22;9:356.

[69] Lawrence D, Mitrou F, Zubrick SR. Smoking and mental illness: results from population surveys in Australia and the United States. *BMC Public Health* 2009 Aug 7;9:285.

[70] Kiviniemi MT, Orom H, Giovino GA. Psychological Distress and Smoking Behavior: The Nature of the Relation Differs by Race/Ethnicity. *Nicotine. Tob. Res.* 2010 Dec 15.

[71] Goodwin RD. Association between physical activity and mental disorders among adults in the United States. *Prev. Med.* 2003 Jun;36(6):698-703.

[72] Dalgard OS. Social inequalities in mental health in Norway: possible explanatory factors. *Int. J. Equity. Health* 2008 Dec 24;7:27.

[73] Ezoe S, Morimoto K. Behavioral lifestyle and mental health status of Japanese factory workers. *Prev. Med.* 1994 Jan;23(1):98-105.

[74] Hamer M, Stamatakis E, Steptoe A. Dose-response relationship between physical activity and mental health: the Scottish Health Survey. *Br. J. Sports. Med.* 2009 Dec;43(14):1111-1114.

[75] Henderson A, Langston V, Greenberg N. Alcohol misuse in the Royal Navy. *Occup .Med.* (Lond) 2009 Jan;59(1):25-31.

[76] Romero MI, Santander J, Hitschfeld MJ, Labbe M, Zamora V. Smoking and alcohol drinking among medical students at the Pontificia Universidad Catolica de Chile]. *Rev. Med. Chil.* 2009 Mar;137(3):361-368.

[77] Saarni SI, Joutsenniemi K, Koskinen S, Suvisaari J, Pirkola S, Sintonen H, et al. Alcohol consumption, abstaining, health utility, and quality of life--a general population survey in Finland. *Alcohol Alcohol* 2008 May-Jun;43(3):376-386.

[78] McElroy SL, Kotwal R, Malhotra S, Nelson EB, Keck PE, Nemeroff CB. Are mood disorders and obesity related? A review for the mental health professional. *J. Clin. Psychiatry.* 2004 May;65(5):634-51, quiz 730.

[79] Veggi AB, Lopes CS, Faerstein E, Sichieri R. Body mass index, body weight perception and common mental disorders among university employees in Rio de Janeiro]. *Rev. Bras. Psiquiatr.* 2004 Dec;26(4):242-247.

[80] Kivimaki M, Lawlor DA, Singh-Manoux A, Batty GD, Ferrie JE, Shipley MJ, et al. Common mental disorder and obesity: insight from four repeat measures over 19 years: prospective Whitehall II cohort study. *BMJ* 2009 Oct 6;339:b3765.

[81] Atlantis E, Baker M. Obesity effects on depression: systematic review of epidemiological studies. *Int. J. Obes.* (Lond) 2008 Jun;32(6):881-891.

[82] Andreyeva T, Puhl RM, Brownell KD. Changes in perceived weight discrimination among Americans, 1995-1996 through 2004-2006. *Obesity. (Silver Spring)* 2008 May;16(5):1129-1134.

[83] Dallman MF, Pecoraro N, Akana SF, La Fleur SE, Gomez F, Houshyar H, et al. Chronic stress and obesity: a new view of "comfort food". *Proc. Natl. Acad. Sci. USA* 2003 Sep 30;100(20):11696-11701.

In: Psychological Distress　　　　　ISBN: 978-1-61942-646-7
Editors: H. Ohayashi and S. Yamada　　© 2012 Nova Science Publishers, Inc.

Chapter 4

UNPAID DOMESTIC WORK AND PSYCHOLOGICAL DISTRESS

Bonnie Janzen and Ivan W. Kelly

University of Saskatchewan, Saskatoon, Canada

ABSTRACT

A large body of research has examined the relationship between work and physical and mental health outcomes, including psychological distress. While the main bulk of this research has addressed paid work, more recently unpaid domestic work (e.g. housework, childrearing) has also been considered. An understanding of the relationship between domestic work and psychological distress has been hindered by a lack of clarity concerning what consistitutes unpaid work, challenges and inconsistencies in measurement, along with a lack of guiding theory. This chapter considers these issues, reports on research conducted to date, and makes recommendations for future research examining unpaid work and psychological distress.

INTRODUCTION

Recent research suggests that time spent on paid work and domestic labor[1] have become more similar between partners over the last four decades in economically developed countries (Kan, Sullivan and Gershuny, 2011). This gradual convergence, however, remains far from complete as women continue to perform more hours of domestic work than men (and men more hours of paid work than women) (Marshall, 2006). A growing body of research has been dedicated to trying to understand the persistence of this gendered division of labor (Lachance-Grzela and Bouchard, 2010) along with, importantly, the long term economic consequences for women (MacDonald, Phipps, and Lethbridge, 2005). Relatively few studies in comparison have studied the potential consequences of unpaid family work for mental health – a state of affairs which is in stark contrast to the voluminous literature dedicated to understanding the impact of paid work on mental health (Stansfeld and Candy, 2006).

This lack of research attention is likely the result of numerous factors, ranging from bias on the part of researchers in considering household labor as "real work" and therefore less worthy of study as a potential determinant of mental health, to the many conceptual and measurement difficulties in attempting to accurately characterize such a complex, often invisible role. This is an important gap to address given the hundreds of hours that North Americans in general, and women in particular, will spend in housework and child rearing over a life time (Kan et al. 2011).

The purpose of this chapter will be to critically review the quantitative research literature that examines the relationship between unpaid domestic work and psychological distress among women. More specifically, this review will highlight: 1) the aspects of unpaid domestic work which have been studied in relation to women's psychological distress; and 2) the conceptual and methodological challenges and limitations of this body of literature which need to be addressed in order to advance the field.

---

[1] Throughout this chapter, the terms "family work", "domestic work", "household work" and "household labor" are used interchangeably.

LITERATURE REVIEW

Unpaid domestic work has been defined in a number of ways in the research literature, though in most studies, the definition must be inferred from how it is measured in that particular study (Coltrane, 2000; Shelton and John, 1996).

As noted by Shelton and John (1996), the most common definition of housework is as "unpaid work done to maintain family members and or a home" (p.300). Researchers may include childcare in their definitions, but often leave out more "invisible" types of work (e.g. emotional work) from their studies.

Similarly, with some exceptions (primarily from the sociological literature) (e.g. Robinson and Spitze, 1992; Bird, 1999; Glass and Fujimoto, 1994), explicitly stated theory regarding how unpaid family work may be related to psychological distress is often neglected in the research literature. More often than not, connections between elements of domestic work and mental health have to be surmised based on relatively vague statements by authors in the introduction/discussion sections of papers and/or according to how unpaid domestic work is measured in their study (for example, the absolute amount of housework performed versus the extent to which household is shared between partners).

Despite this limitation, several explanations can be gleaned from the literature which link unpaid domestic work with mental health outcomes. These are: 1) the role strain perspective; 2) the division of household labor; and 3) the psychosocial work environment.

Role Strain

The starting point for much research in the area of unpaid domestic work and mental health is the view of domestic work as an inherently negative activity (Lennon, 1994; Robinson and Spitze, 1992). This perspective of family work is consistent with the broader context of women's health research. That is, despite overwhelming evidence of the mental and physical health enhancing effects of multiple role occupancy for many women (McMunn, Bartley, Hardy, and Kuh, 2006), the majority of research continues to implicitly or explicitly adopt a role strain perspective (Barnett and Hyde, 2001). This approach focuses on the premise that human energy is limited, and the more demands within a role, or the more roles a person occupies, the more strain experienced and the greater the likelihood of negative effects on mental health (Goode, 1960). Thus, more time and effort spent in housework and child rearing may create role overload, particularly if combined with paid work, resulting in time pressure and subsequent psychological distress.

A variety of measures have been employed to assess the burdens of domestic work. Some research has relied on household structural variables as proxy indicators domestic workload, such as household size, children's age or the presence of older adults (Artazcoz et al. 2001; Regidor, Pascual, de la Fuente, Santos, Astasio, and Ortega, 2010). Given the lack of specificity of these variables, it is perhaps not surprising that these indicators have been inconsistently related to women's psychological distress (Matthews and Powers, 2002; Artazcoz, 2001). Time use measures are an alternative operationalization of domestic workload level. Although some studies have relied on time diary data (Hook, 2006), most family work studies with mental health as an outcome have used direct questions; these require respondents to estimate how much time they usually spend per day or week on specific domestic work tasks (Boye, 2010, Glass and Fujimoto, 1994). However, more time spent on domestic work has not been associated with women's mental health in a predictable way. That is, some research has found more time spent in family work to be associated with poorer mental health (Vaananen, Kevin, Ala-Mursula, Pentti, Kivimaki, and Vahtera, 2004; Glass and Fujimoto, 1994), other studies have found more family work to be unrelated to mental health (Harryson, Novo, and Hammarstrom, 2010; Escriba-Aguir and Tenias-Burillo, 2004; Robinson and Spitze, 1992; Voydanoff, 1999) or even associated with better mental health (but only up to a particular threshold of hours, after which more time spent in housework is associated with an increase in psychological distress) (Boye, 2010). Glass and Fujimoto (1994) however found no evidence of a non-linear association between time in housework and psychological distress. Yet other research has found more time spent in domestic labor to be associated with poorer mental health but only for particular subgroups of women, such as employed women with lower education levels (Artazcoz et al. 2004), blue-collar workers (Asztalos et al., 2009) or women with stressful jobs (Mellner, Krantz, and Lundberg, 2006). Hence, no consistent findings have emerged within the role strain perspective.

Household Division of Labor

A second explanation linking domestic work and psychological distress focuses, not on the absolute amount of work done, but rather, on the proportion of family work done relative to one's partner (Glass and Fujimoto, 1994). According to equity theory, couples evaluate both what they put into a relationship and what they get out of a relationship; equity between partners is attained when both contribute and benefit fairly within the relationship (Thompson, 1991). The division of family work is one area that can contribute to couples' perceptions of equity or inequity in a relationship, and thus potentially impact psychological well-being. In the case of household labor, equity theory predicts that those partners who perform an equitable share will be less psychologically distressed than either those who perform a disproportionately small or large share, the latter being associated with the greatest likelihood of psychological distress.

Various measures have been applied to assess the household division of labor. "Objective" measures involve obtaining an estimate of hours of domestic work from both partners and dividing each respondent's housework hours by the total number reported by both partners (Glass and Fujimoto, 1994; Bird, 1999) or having respondents rate their domestic responsibilities on an ordinal scale, from no responsibility to total responsibility (Matthews and Powers, 2002). Several studies using such objective measures of equity have reported that the more proportionate time women spend in household labour relative to their partner, the greater their level of depression or psychological distress (Harryson, Novo, Hammarstrom, 2010; Khawaja and Habib, 2007), whereas other studies have reported no such relationship (Barnett and Shen, 1997; Boye, 2010; Goldberg and Perry-Jenkins, 2004). Bird (1999) reported a curvilinear relationship between contribution to housework and psychological distress; that is, among employed women, performing an increasing proportion of the housework was associated with lower psychological distress but only until a particular point (ie., 50%) after which psychological distress began to increase. Boye (2010) however, failed to replicate this association. Goldberg and Perry-Jenkins (2004) claim that understanding of the relationship between family work and mental health has been impeded by the tendency of researchers to only include measures of housework *or* to combine questions on child rearing and housework into one measure, so that the independent associations of each with mental health, if present, cannot be determined. The few studies which have considered child rearing and housework separately suggest that an unequal division of child rearing may be more strongly associated with women's psychological distress than an unequal division of housework (Des Rivieres-Pigeon, Saurel-Cubizolles, and Romito, 2002; Matthews and Power, 2002; Tao, Janzen and Abonyi, 2010). In addition, although women's actions directed toward improving the emotional and psychological well-being of family members (ie., emotional labour) has not been traditionally included in domestic work research, increasing evidence suggests that more time spent in emotional work relative to one's partner is associated with higher levels of depression among women in dual-earner families (Stranzdins and Broom, 2004).

In addition to the type of task, whether one *perceives* the division of family work as fair or unfair may also be relevant to understanding the relationship between household labor and psychological distress (Claffey and Manning, 2010). Performing a disproportionate amount of the family work does not invariably result in perceptions of unfairness (Lennon and Rosenfeld, 1994). Subjective measures of the household division of labor involve asking respondents how fair he/she perceives the amount of paid or domestic labor undertook relative to their partner's contribution, with typical response options being: 1=very unfair to me, 2=somewhat unfair to me, 3=fair to both, 4 =somewhat unfair to partner, 5 = very unfair to partner) (Glass and Fujimoto, 1994). A growing body of research has focused on identifying factors associated with perceptions of fairness; that is, understanding why a considerable proportion of women perform the bulk of domestic work and view the division as fair (Braun, Lewin-Epstein, Stier, and Baumgartner, 2008; Greenstein, 2009). At the same time, relatively few studies have focused on the potential mental health consequences of perceived unfairness in household work. The limited research which does exist suggests a positive association between perceived unfairness in the division of family work and depressive symptoms (Claffey and Mickelson, 2009; Robinson and Spitze, 1992; Voydanoff and Donnelly, 1999).

Psychosocial Work Environment

Drawing upon the paid work literature which suggests that the psychological and social conditions of work vary greatly among the employed and in ways which impact mental health (Stansfeld and Candy, 2006), another body of research has examined the relationship between the psychosocial quality of unpaid domestic work and mental health outcomes. The psychosocial environment refers to "*the sociostructural range of opportunities that is available to an individual person to meet his or her needs of well being, productivity and positive self-experience"* (Seigrist and Marmot, 2004, p. 1465). Schooler and colleagues (1984) hypothesized that people engaged in domestic work that requires intellectual activity, task variety, and authority over their work would have better psychological health than those participating in monotonous work that was lacking in cognitive challenge and control. Most research examining the relationship between the psychosocial quality of domestic work and psychological distress has been based on Karasek's and Theorell's (1990) job strain model. Within this framework, workers' psychological job demands (e.g., pace, effort, volume) interact with their level of decision latitude (e.g. ability to make decisions at work and opportunity to use skills) to determine the psychosocial quality of their work. Job strain occurs when the psychological demands of the job are high and the worker's decision latitude (ie., job control) is low. Others have conceptualized the psychosocial quality of domestic work as the difference between the rewarding aspects of the work (e.g. being able to set one's own standards) and that concerning unrewarding aspects of the work (e.g. being bored by the routine)(Kibria, Barnett, Baruch, Marshall, and Pleck, 1990; Walters et al. 1996). To assess the psychosocial quality of unpaid family work, many researchers have developed their own study-specific, typically multi-item scales (Kushnir and Malamed, 2006; Staland-Nyman, Alexanderson, and Hensing, 2008; Kibria et al., 1990; Lennon, 1994; Walters et al. 1996), none of which have been universally adopted within the field.

Research indicates that the psychosocial characteristics of women's unpaid family work do vary appreciably and in ways which are associated with their mental health. For example, higher levels of depression, anxiety, and burnout have been found among women reporting domestic work characterized as highly demanding (Peeter, Montgomery, Bakker, and Schaufeli, 2005; Kushnir and Malamed, 2006; Lennon, 1994; Schooler et al. 1984; Walters et al. 1996), routine (Lennon, 1994) or lacking in substantive complexity (ie., degree to which performance of the work requires thought and independent judgment) (Schooler et al. 1984). Control over work activities has been identified as particularly critical for promoting mental health in the paid work environment (Siegrist and Marmot, 2004) and the concept has become an increasing foci in the domestic work and health literature (Chandola et al. 2004; Griffin et al., 2002). For example, Barnett and Shen (1997, p. 2) categorized various domestic tasks in terms of schedule control, that is, one's *"ability to schedule tasks to reflect one's personal needs rather than having to perform the tasks on a schedule independent of one's personal needs"*. Low-schedule-control tasks, such as laundry and cooking, are those which must typically be done every day and at certain times, with the worker experiencing very little discretion in the scheduling of tasks. In contrast, high-schedule-control tasks, such as yard work and car maintenance, are often initiated and completed according to the worker's preference and can often be performed without any time urgency. The performance of high- and low-schedule-control activities is highly gendered within households, with women typically spending more hours on low-schedule-control tasks and men on high-schedule-control tasks (Kan et al. 2011). Barnett and Shen (1997) found for both husbands and wives, more time spent performing low-schedule-control tasks was associated with greater distress, whereas the amount of time spent on high-schedule-control tasks was unrelated to mental health outcomes, though Robinson and Spitze (1992) failed to find such an association. Although it is often assumed in the literature that it is the low schedule control domestic activities that are most harmful to psychological well-being (Coltrane, 2000), little research was found which has systematically tested this hypothesis. This gap in knowledge is important to address, particularly given recent research suggesting that although couple's paid and unpaid work hours are slowly converging over time, the least amount of convergence has been observed with respect to low schedule control housework tasks (e.g. cleaning, laundry), the bulk of which is still performed by women (Kan et al. 2011).

It is important to note that the conceptualization of control in the domestic work literature still remains preliminary, with little clarity regarding the key components which are most important for understanding women's mental health (Kushnir and Melamed, 2006). While some researchers, like Barnett and Shen (1997), have focused on aspects of control which have been similarly defined and measured in the paid work literature (Staland-Nyman et al. 2008; Lombardi and Ulrich, 1997), others point to the uniqueness of the home environment and the need for revised concepts and measures which reflect that uniqueness. For example, Kushnir and Melamed (2006) developed a measure of shared control in family-related decision-making, and though unrelated to measures of burnout among employed mothers, was associated with life satisfaction. Others point out the need to clarify whether control in the domestic environment is best conceptualized in terms of women's degree of access (or lack of access) to resources needed to successfully cope with family demands or control in terms of power (ie., decision making ability) within the household (Griffin et al. 2002; Chandola, 2004). Although Griffin et al. (2002) found women (and men) who perceived themselves as having low control in the home environment to be at greater risk of depression, the single item measure of control used in the study precluded the ability to make nuanced interpretations.

DISCUSSION AND CONCLUSION

The study of occupational exposures and their mental health effects has been an important research focus within the health and social sciences for many years. Although the early emphasis of this research was on men, an understanding of the qualities and characteristics of paid work which impact women's mental health has increased greatly over the last two decades, though gaps remain (Artazcoz, Borrell, Cortas, Escriba-Aguir, and Cascant, 2007). In contrast to paid work, relatively little is known about the characteristics of unpaid family work which may influence mental health. But what does the research that has been conducted say? That is, is unpaid domestic work among women associated with psychological distress? Unfortunately, research on this topic has, to date, produced equivocal findings: some studies say yes (Glass and Fujimoto, 1994), other studies say no (Goldberg and Perry-Jenkins, 2004), and even more say "it depends" (Artazcoz et al. 2004; Asztalos et al., 2009). Unfortunately what "it" depends upon is not at all consistent across studies. While this review of the literature does suggest that, all in all, unpaid work can be detrimental to women's mental health, it is difficult to clearly articulate under what conditions such a relationship would hold. Adding to interpretative challenges is that with a few exceptions (e.g. Harryson et al., 2010; Goldberg and Perry-Jenkins, 2004), most research has been conducted cross-sectionally, making it difficult to tease out the actual direction of association between unpaid domestic work and psychological distress.

Disparate research findings themselves are likely the result of numerous factors. Lack of consistency across studies in what constitutes unpaid domestic work is a likely contributory factor (e.g. housework, child-rearing or both), as is the diversity of measures used. In addition, study participants have varied widely between studies in terms of age, stage in the family life course, employment status, and family role characteristics. Family and paid work responsibilities and resources vary considerably throughout the adult life course in ways which may impact the division of family work, the psychosocial quality of the work, and thus, the potential impact of that work on mental health (Marshall, 2011). Inconsistent adjustment of covariates in multivariate models also likely contributes to disparate research findings.

Others have questioned whether current quantitative measures of domestic work actually encompass the "essence" of unpaid domestic work (Warren, 2011; Walters et al. 2002). After all, family labor is complex, often invisible, characterized by some as , "...*largely mental, spread over time, and mixed in with other activities, often looking like other things*" (Mederer, 1993, p. 135). Following a review of quantitative research examining unpaid work in the UK over the past decade, Warren (2011) concluded that many of these studies were based on data sets which failed to adequately reflect the complexities of unpaid work, such as "*domestic work practices (who does what); relationships (for, from and with whom); negotiations (how); and meanings of domestic work (for those carrying out domestic work and others)*" (p. 132). Canadian researchers have similarly drawn attention to the lack of quality information on domestic work contained in large scale government health surveys, such as Statistic's Canada's National Population Health Surveys and the Canadian Community Health Surveys (Walters et al. 2002), thus having to rely on superficial indicators of family workload such as the number and ages of children. To address the measurement deficiencies of large scale government surveys, a number of researchers over the last several decades have developed their own measurement scales to assess various qualities of family work (e.g. Lombardi and Ulbrich, 1997; Lennon, 1994; Walters et al. 1996; Kushnir and Melamed, 2006; Staland-Nyman et al. 2008). Certainly, some interesting relationships are emerging from this body of work, such as those between perceptions of control (Griffin et al. 2002) and demands (Peeter et al. 2005) within the domestic environment and women's risk of psychological distress. Unfortunately, none of these measures appear to have undergone rigorous scale development procedures nor do they appear to have been used on more than one occasion or by more than one researcher.

Clearly articulated theory is critical for the development of valid and reliable measures. Although expressed a decade ago, this review of the literature suggests that the opinion voiced by Walters and colleagues (2002) still applies today: "*Research on work within the home is still in its infancy. We do not have conceptual frameworks which are as well developed as in the case of paid work, nor are the elements of domestic labor clearly identified*" (p.679). Nor is it clearly and consistently articulated in the literature as to why (and how) unpaid domestic work should be related to psychological distress. As recently observed, "*...without careful attention to theory and building models that are empirically testable, research results can be interpreted in any fashion, full of the influence of biases, proclivities, ideologies, and possibly* *even ignorance. The theory building process not only helps to keep us honest, it helps us progress"* (Carpiano and Daley, 2006, p. 567).

REFERENCES

Artazcoz, L., Borrell, C., and Benach, J. (2001). Gender inequalities in health among workers: The relation with family demands. *Journal of Epidemiology and Community Health, 55,* 639-647.

Artazcoz, L., Borrell, C., Benach, J., Cortes, I., and Rohlfs, I. (2004). Women, family demands and health: The importance of employment status and socio-economic position. *Social Science and Medicine, 59,* 263-274.

Artazcoz, L., Borrell, C., Cortas, I., Escriba-Aguir, V., and Cascant, L (2007). Occupational epidemiology and work related inequalities in health: a gender perspective for two complementary approaches to work and health research. *Journal of Epidemiology and Community Health, 61,* 39-45.

Asztalos, M., Wijndaele, K., De Bourdeaudhuij, I., Phillippaerts, R., Matton, L., et al. (2009). Specific associations between types of physical activity and components of mental health. *Journal of Science and Medicine in Sport, 12,* 468-474.

Barnett, R., and Hyde, J. (2001). Women, men, work and family. An expansionist theory.*American Psychologist, 56,* 781–96.

Barnett, R. C., and Shen, Y. C. (1997). Gender, high- and low-schedule-control housework tasks, and psychological distress - a study of dual-earner couples. *Journal of Family Issues, 18,* 403-428.

Bird, C. E. (1999). Gender, household labor, and psychological distress: The impact of the amount and division of housework. *Journal of Health and Social Behavior, 40,* 32-45.

Boye, K. (2010). Time spent working. Paid work, housework and the gender difference in psychological distress. *European Societies, 12,* 419-442.

Braun, M., Lewin-Epstein, N., Stier, H., and Baumgartner, M. (2008). Perceived equity in the gendered division of household labor. *Journal of Marriage and Family, 70,* 1145-1156.

Carpiano, R., and Daley, D. (2006). A guide and glossary on postpositivist theory building for population health. *Journal of Epidemiology and Community Health, 60,* 564-570.

Chandola, T., Kuper, H., Singh-Manoux, A., Bartley, M., and Marmot, M. (2004). The effect of control at home on CHD events in the Whitehall II study: Gender differences in psychosocial domestic pathways to social inequalities in CHD. *Social Science and Medicine, 58*, 1501-1509.

Claffey, S., and Mickelson, K. (2009). Division of household labor and distress: The role of perceived fairness for employed mothers. *Sex Roles, 60*, 819-831.

Claffey, S., and Manning, K. (2010). Equity by not equality: Commentary on Lachance-Grzela and Bouchard. *Sex Roles, 63*, 781-785.

Coltrane, S. (2000). Research on household labor: Modeling and measuring the social embeddedness of routine family work. *Journal of Marriage and Family, 62*, 1208-33.

Des Rivieres-Pigeon, C., Saurel-Cubizolles, M. J., and Romito, P. (2002). Division of domestic work and psychological distress 1 year after childbirth: A comparison between France, Quebec and Italy. *Journal of Community and Applied Social Psychology, 12,* 397-409.

Escriba-Aguir, V., and Tenias-Burillo, J. (2004). Psychological well-being among hospital personnel: The role of family demands and psychosocial work environment. *International Archives of Occupational and Environmental Health, 77*, 401-408.

Glass, J., and Fujimoto, T. (1994). Housework, paid work, and depression among husbands and wives. *Journal of Health and Social Behavior, 35,* 179-191.

Goldberg, A. E., and Perry-Jenkins, M. (2004). Division of labor and working-class women's well-being across the transition to parenthood. *Journal of Family Psychology, 18,* 225-236.

Goode, W. (1960). A theory of role strain. *American Sociological Review, 25,* 483-496.Greinstein, T. (2009). National context, family satisfaction, and fairness in the division of household labor. *Journal of Marriage and Family, 71*, 1039-1051.

Griffin, J. M., Fuhrer, R., Stansfeld, S. A., and Marmot, M. (2002). The importance of low control at work and home on depression and anxiety: Do these effects vary by gender and social class? *Social Science and Medicine, 54,* 783-798.

Harryson, L., Novo, M., and Hammarstrom, A. (2010). Is gender inequality in the domestic sphere associated with psychological distress among women and men? Results from the Northern Swedish Cohort. *Journal of Epidemiology and Community Health.* Published Online First: 12 October 2010.

Hook, J. L. (2006). Care in context: men's unpaid work in 20 countries, 1965-2003. *American Sociological Review, 71*, 639-660.

Kan, M., Sullivan, O., and Gershuny, J. (2011). Gender convergence in domestic work: Discerning the effects of interactional and institutional barriers from large-scale data. *Sociology, 45*, 234-251.

Karasek, R., Brisson, C., Kawakami, N., Houtman, I., Bongers, P., and Amick, B. (1998). The Job Content Questionnaire: An instrument for internationally comparative assessments of psychosocial job characteristics. *Journal of Occupational Health Psychology, 3*, 322-355.

Karasek, R., and Theorell, T. (1990). *Healthy work: Stress, productivity and the reconstruction of working life*. New York: Basic Books.

Khawaja, M., and Habib, R. (2007). Husbands' involvement in housework and women's psychosocial health: Findings from a population-based study in Lebanon. *American Journal of Public Health, 97*, 860-866.

Kibria, N., Barnett, R. C., Baruch, G. K., Marshall, N. L., and Pleck, J. H. (1990). Homemaking-role quality and the psychological well-being and distress of employed women. *Sex Roles, 22*, 327-347.

Krantz, G., Berntsson, L., and Lundberg, U. (2005). Total workload, work stress, and perceived symptoms in Swedish male and female white-collar employees. *The European Journal of Public Health, 15*, 209-214.

Kushnir, T., and Melamed, S. (2006). Domestic stress and well-being of employed women: Interplay between demands and decision control at home. *Sex Roles, 54*, 687-694.

Lachance-Grzela, M., and Bouchard, G. (2010). Why do women do the lion's share of housework? A decade of research. *Sex Roles, 63*, 767-780.

Lennon, M. C. (1994). Women, work, and well-being: The importance of work conditions. *Journal of Health and Social Behavior, 35*, 235-247.

Lombardi, E., and Ulbrich, P. (1997). Work conditions, mastery and psychological distress: Are housework and paid work contexts conceptually similar? *Women and Health, 26*, 17-39.

MacDonald, M., Phipps, S., and Lethbridge, L. (2005). Taking its toll: The influence of paid and unpaid work on women's well-being. *Feminist Economics, 11*, 63-94.

Marshall, K. (2006). Converging gender roles. *Perspectives on Labor and Income, 7*, 5-17.

Matthews, S., and Power, C. (2002). Socio-economic gradients in psychological distress: A focus on women, social roles and work-home characteristics. *Social Science and Medicine, 54*, 799-810.

Matthews, S., Power, C., and Stansfeld, S. A. (2001). Psychological distress and work and home roles: A focus on socio-economic differences in distress. *Psychological medicine, 31*, 725-736.

McMunn, A., Bartley, M., Hardy, R., and Kuh, D. (2006). Life course social roles and women's health in mid-life: Causation or selection? *Journal of Epidemiology and Community Health, 60*, 484-489.

Mederer, H. J. (1993). Division of labor in two-earner homes-task accomplishment versus household management as critical variables in perceptions about family work. *Journal of Marriage and the Family, 55*, 133-145.

Mellner, C., Krantz, G., and Lundberg, U. (2006). Symptom reporting and self-rated health among women in mid-life: The role of work characteristics and family responsibilities. *International Journal of Behavioural Medicine, 13*, 1-7.

Nordenmark, M., and Nyman, C. (2003). Fair or unfair? Perceived fairness of household division of labour and gender equality among women and men: The Swedish case. *European Journal of Women's Studies, 10*, 181-209.

Peeters, M., Montgomery, A., Bakker, A., and Schaufeli, W. (2005). Balancing work and home: How job and home demands are related to burnout. *International Journal of Stress Management, 12*, 43–61.

Regidor, E., Pascual, C., de la Fuente, L., Santos, J., Astasio, P., et al. (2010). Socio-economic position, family demands and reported health in working men and women. *European Journal of Public Health, 21*, 109-115.

Robinson, J., and Spitze, G. (1992). Whistle while you work - the effect of household task-performance on women's and men's well-being. *Social Science Quarterly, 73*, 844-861.

Schooler, C., Miller, J., Miller, K. A., and Richtand, C. N. (1984). Work for the household - its nature and consequences for husbands and wives. *American Journal of Sociology, 90*, 97-124.

Shelton, B. A., and John, D (1996). The division of household labor. *Annual Review of Sociology, 22*, 299-322.

Siegrist, J., and Marmot, M. (2004). Health inequalities and the psychosocial environment – two scientific challenges. *Social Science and Medicine, 58*, 1463-1473.

Staland Nyman, C., Alexanderson, K., and Hensing, G (2008). Associations between strain in domestic work and self-rated health: A study of employed women in Sweden. *Scandanavian Journal of Public Health, 36*, 21-27.

Stansfeld, S., and Candy, B. (2006). Psychosocial work environment and mental health - A meta-analytic review. *Scandinavian Journal of Work, Environment, and Health, 32*, 443-462.

Strazdins, L., and Broom, D. (2004). Acts of love (and work). Gender imbalance in emotional work and women's psychological distress. *Journal of Family Issues, 25,* 356-378.

Tao, W., Janzen, B., and Abonyi, S. (2010). Gender, division of unpaid family work, and psychological distress in dual-earner families. *Clinical Practice and Epidemiology in Mental Health, 6,* 36-46.

Thompson, L. (1991). Family work: Women's sense of equity and of fairness. *Journal of Family Issues, 12,* 181-96.

Vaananen, A., Kevin, M., Ala-Mursula, L., et al. (2004). The double burden of and negative spillover between paid and domestic work: Associations with health among men and women. *Women and Health, 40,* 1-18.

Voydanoff, P., and Donnelly, B. (1999). The intersection of time in activities and perceived unfairness in relation to psychological distress and marital quality. *Journal of Marriage and Family, 61,* 739-51.

Walters, V., McDonough, P., and Strohschein, L. (2002). The influence of work, household structure, and social, personal and material resources on gender differences in health: An analysis of the 1994 Canadian National Population Health Survey. *Social Science and Medicine,54,* 677-92.

Walters, V., Lenton, R., French, S., Eyles, J., Mayr, J., and Newbold, B. (1996). Paid work, unpaid work and social support: A study of the health of male and female nurses. *Social Science and Medicine, 43,* 1627-1636.

Warren, T. (2011). Researching the gender division of unpaid domestic work: Practices, relationships, negotiations, and meanings. *The Sociological Review, 59,* 129-148.

In: Psychological Distress   ISBN: 978-1-61942-646-7
Editors: H. Ohayashi and S. Yamada   © 2012 Nova Science Publishers, Inc.

Chapter 5

RELATIONSHIPS AMONG THE KESSLER 10 PSYCHOLOGICAL DISTRESS SCALE, SOCIO-DEMOGRAPHIC STATUS, EMPLOYMENT-RELATED VARIABLES, AND INTERNALITY-EXTERNALITY IN JAPANESE EMPLOYEES

*Masahito Fushimi**

Akita Prefectural Mental Health and Welfare Center,
2-1-51 Nakadori, Akita City, Akita Prefecture, Japan
Akita Occupational Health Promotion Center,
Akita City, Akita Prefecture, Japan

ABSTRACT

Among developed nations, Japan has one of the world's highest suicide rates. Mental health problems such as anxiety or depressive disorders are considered major public health issues, given that the likelihood of suicide is linked to these disorders. The aim of this study was to examine the prevalence of and factors related to psychological distress among employees in Japan. Employees from Akita prefecture in Japan were invited to complete self-administered questionnaires based on the Kessler 10 (K10) psychological distress scale. A value of 22 or higher

---

* Correspondence should be addressed to Masahito Fushimi (fushimi@pref.akita.lg.jp; fushimi@sings.jp).

on the K10 scale indicated high or very high levels of psychological distress. Furthermore, we identified the relationships among the K10 psychological distress scale, socio-demographic status (sex, age, and education), employment-related variables (full-/part-time work, managerial class, job category, and working hours), and individual personality traits regarding internality-externality (locus of control scale). Analysis of data from 1,512 employees (males: 624; females: 888) indicated that the mean score and standard deviation of the K10 scores was 20.23 ± 8.04 (males: 19.52 ± 8.19; females: 20.74 ± 7.90), and that 37.2% of the employees (males: 33.7%; females: 39.6%) had high or very high levels of psychological distress ($\geq$ 22 of the K10 scores). The mean scores and proportion of psychological distress on the K10 scale found in the present study were high as compared to those found in previous studies. The results of Pearson's χ^2 test based on the K10 scale regarding sex ($p < 0.05$), age ($p < 0.001$), education ($p < 0.05$), and job category ($p < 0.001$) showed significant differences between high or very high levels of psychological distress group ($\geq$ 22 of the K10 scores), and the others. Furthermore, multiple regression analyses indicated significant effects in the K10 scale with respect to age, education, job category, and the locus of control scale. Data from this study can be used as K10 benchmark values to enhance the significance of future corporate health risk appraisal surveys. The results of this study may therefore help improve the understanding of psychological distress in employees.

INTRODUCTION

Comprehensive large-scale mental health epidemiological studies in several countries have concluded that the prevalence of mental health problems in a society is quite common [1–5]. Japan has one of the highest suicide rates among developed countries, and mental health problems are blamed for the majority of reported suicides. Thus, issues related to mental health are of significant concern for the country [6–8]. In general, major epidemiological studies pertaining to mental health utilize complex, interviewer-administered diagnostic surveys, and replicating this technique is considered to be economically unfeasible for employers. Occupational safety and health (OSH) programs typically invite employees to complete a voluntary health assessment questionnaire consisting of brief self-report health scales at the workplace. The Kessler 10 (K10) is a brief, well-validated scale that assesses psychological distress and effectively predicts mental disorders [7–9]. In this study, the K10 scale was employed to assess the psychological distress of employees.

It is important to employ a proactive health screening mechanism to identify stressful situations and stress management skills of employees. Several previous studies on stress have explored the relationship between stressors and psychological distress. In addition, several such studies adopted moderators as factors, one of them being the locus of control (LOC) scale. This factor serves as a potential moderator of the relationship between the stressor and psychological distress, and is synonymous with internality-externality [10–13]. The LOC refers to the differences in beliefs concerning personal control, represented by the continuum from internality to externality. "Internals" believe that "reinforcements are contingent upon their own behavior, capacities, or attributes." In contrast, "externals" believe that "reinforcements are not under their personal control, but rather are under the control of powerful others, luck, chance, fate, etc" [10]. Therefore, the LOC scale may affect the long-term coping pattern of individuals. In order to understand the processes related to occupational stress, it is necessary to explore how individuals behave in response to perceived stress (i.e., coping behavior). However, not all coping takes place only during stressful incidents or episodes. Therefore, it is important to study the long-term pattern of coping behavior (i.e., coping style), because psychological distress builds up over months or years, rather than as a mere response to a single stressful incident. Consequently, this study does not focus on individual stressful incidents, but rather on the coping style, which is assessed by the LOC scale.

MATERIALS AND METHODS

Participants

The information presented in this report was collected as part of the Akita Occupational Health Promotion Center's Study for Mental Health [7, 8, 13]. The participants in this study were recruited as follows. Randomly selected employers were selected (through random systematic sampling), and their employees were invited to complete a self-administered questionnaire during a one-month survey period (September–October 2007). In all, fifteen employers from public and private sector firms in Akita prefecture, Japan, agreed to participate in the study. The questionnaires were distributed to the participants using paper-based methods. In addition, this study obtained socio-demographic information from the participants. The demographic information collected during this study included sex, age distribution (29 years or younger,

30 to 39 years, 40 to 49 years, and 50 years and older), and the highest level of education obtained (compulsory or senior high school, tertiary education, and graduate degree or higher). The questionnaire survey also elicited information on the employees' occupational characteristics (i.e., full time work, managerial class, job category, and average number of working hours per day). They were asked to select their job category from the following possible choices: (1) clerical or administrative support, (2) sales- or service-related occupation, (3) professional or technical support, and (4) others. Participation in the survey was voluntary and confidential. The Japan Labour Health and Welfare Organization, which has established occupational health promotion centers in each administrative division, approved the study protocol.

Instruments

K10 Scale

As mentioned above, the current study administered the K10 scale (30-day prevalence) to assess psychological distress. The psychological dimensions explored in K10 make it sensitive and specific to mental disorders like affective and anxiety disorders [7–9]. Each of the 10 items on the K10 scale is rated on a 5-point scale ranging from "none of the time" (value = 1) to "all of the time" (value = 5). The sum of the response scores can range from 10 to 50. Previous studies of the K10 indicate that scores between 30 and 50 represent very high psychological distress; scores between 22 and 29 indicate high psychological distress; scores between 16 and 21 indicate moderate psychological distress; and scores between 10 and 15 represent low psychological distress [14, 15]. The present study was divided into two categories of psychological distress: high or very high psychological distress (22–50) and the others (10–21).

LOC Scale

In this study, the LOC scale was used to measure individual personality traits; namely, the internality-externality of the participant. Instead of using the original LOC scale developed by Rotter [10], Kambara and his colleagues developed an alternative measure of the LOC [16, 17]. They named their 18-item scale (9-items each for internality and externality) the "Japanese version of the LOC scale." Each item is evaluated using a 4-point rating scale ranging from "value = 1" to "value = 4." The respondent is instructed to indicate a degree of agreement or disagreement with each item on the 4-point scale.

Therefore, the sum of the response scores can range from 18 to 72, with higher scores indicating internality. In the previous study quoted here, internal consistency reliability was estimated at 0.78, and the test-retest reliability was 0.76 [16, 17]. The current study used this scale. Further information about this scale can be found in Kambara et al [16].

Analytical Procedure

Statistical analyses using cross tabulations of the prevalence of psychological distress versus socio-demographic and employment variables, were performed using SPSS version 11.0J for Windows (SPSS, Tokyo, Japan). Statistical differences for cross tabulations in each category were measured using Pearson's χ^2 statistic. The Mann-Whitney U test was also used to measure the statistical differences with regard to the values of the K10 scale in each category. The correlations between the K10 scale and LOC scale in sex and age distribution were analyzed using Spearman's rank correlation. Furthermore, stepwise multiple regression analyses were performed to assess the effects of related factors. Three regression analyses with the dependent variable as the K10 scale were performed. In one regression, sex was included as an independent variable. The remaining two regressions were conducted on separate data sets for males and females.

RESULTS

Of the 2,145 employees, 1,873 responded to the questionnaire (response rate: 87.3%); however, the number of questionnaires with satisfactory responses, excluding those with insufficient data, was 1,512 (70.5%), which included 624 males and 888 females.

Table 1 divides the participants according to their sex, and summarizes information pertaining to socio-demographic status and employment-related variables. With regard to the differences between males and females, Pearson's χ^2 test revealed significant differences ($p < 0.001$) in age, education, employee type (managerial class), job category, and working hours per day. However, there was no significant difference in employment status (full-time/part-time work).

Table 1. Socio-demographic status and employment-related variables of the sample and the differences between the males and females

	Overall (N=1512)		Male (N=624)		Female (N=888)	
	N	(%)	N	(%)	N	(%)
Age *						
-29	332	(22.0)	115	(18.4)	217	(24.4)
30-39	411	(27.2)	152	(24.4)	259	(29.2)
40-49	395	(26.1)	151	(24.2)	244	(27.5)
50-	374	(24.7)	206	(33.0)	168	(18.9)
Education *						
Compulsory/senior high school	699	(46.2)	426	(68.3)	273	(30.7)
Tertiary education	696	(46.0)	126	(20.2)	570	(64.2)
Graduate degree or higher	97	(6.4)	61	(9.8)	36	(4.1)
Unknown	20	(1.3)	11	(1.8)	9	(1.0)
Employment status						
Full-time work	1342	(88.8)	562	(90.1)	780	(87.8)
Part-time work	158	(10.4)	58	(9.3)	100	(11.3)
Unknown	12	(0.8)	4	(0.6)	8	(0.9)
Employee type *						
Managerial class	161	(10.6)	110	(17.6)	51	(5.7)
Non-managerial class	1329	(87.9)	511	(81.9)	818	(92.1)
Unknown	22	(1.5)	3	(0.5)	19	(2.1)
Job category *						
Clerical/administrative	204	(13.5)	109	(17.5)	95	(10.7)
Sales/service	171	(11.3)	100	(16.0)	71	(8.0)
Professional/technical	773	(51.1)	213	(34.1)	560	(63.1)
Others (on-site workers, etc.)	314	(20.8)	177	(28.4)	137	(15.4)
Unknown	50	(3.3)	25	(4.0)	25	(2.8)
Working hours per day *						
8 hours or less	814	(53.8)	255	(40.9)	559	(63.0)
More than 8 hours	687	(45.4)	366	(58.7)	321	(36.1)
Unknown	11	(0.7)	3	(0.5)	8	(0.9)

Significances representing the differences between males and females (Pearson's χ^2 statistic). * $p < 0.001$.

Table 2 presents the mean scores and standard deviations of the K10 scale on the basis of sex and age distribution. For all age groups, except the 30–39 years group, the mean K10 scores of females were higher than those of males. Furthermore, the older age groups tended to have lower K6 scores, with the exception of the males in the 30–39 years age group. Significant sex-based differences were observed in the 29 years or younger age group ($p < 0.01$), 50 years and older ($p < 0.01$), and all age groups ($p < 0.001$; Mann-Whitney U test).

Table 2. Mean and standard deviations of the Kessler 10 (K10) scores by sex and age distribution

Age	Overall Mean	±	SD	Male Mean	±	SD	Female Mean	±	SD
-29 *	21.36	±	8.25	19.97	±	8.64	22.09	±	7.96
30-39	20.90	±	8.37	21.16	±	8.89	20.74	±	8.06
40-49	20.16	±	7.98	19.94	±	8.24	20.30	±	7.83
50- *	18.58	±	7.28	17.74	±	6.99	19.62	±	7.50
Total **	20.23	±	8.04	19.52	±	8.19	20.74	±	7.90

Significance scores representing the differences between males and females (Mann-Whitney U test). * $p < 0.01$, ** $p < 0.001$.

Table 3. Distribution of the Kessler 10 scores according to four categories of psychological distress (low, moderate, high, and very high) based on gender and age distribution

Age	Overall N L	M	H	VH	% L	M	H	VH
-29	89	103	84	56	26.8	31.0	25.3	16.9
30-39	132	110	110	59	32.1	26.8	26.8	14.4
40-49	130	119	89	57	32.9	30.1	22.5	14.4
50-	150	117	74	33	40.1	31.3	19.8	8.8
Total	501	449	357	205	33.1	29.7	23.6	13.6
Male N L	M	H	VH	% L	M	H	VH	
42	35	19	19	36.5	30.4	16.5	16.5	
52	37	38	25	34.2	24.3	25.0	16.4	
52	42	35	22	34.4	27.8	23.2	14.6	
92	62	38	14	44.7	30.1	18.4	6.8	
238	176	130	80	38.1	28.2	20.8	12.8	
Female N L	M	H	VH	% L	M	H	VH	
47	68	65	37	21.7	31.3	30.0	17.1	
80	73	72	34	30.9	28.2	27.8	13.1	
78	77	54	35	32.0	31.6	22.1	14.3	
58	55	36	19	34.5	32.7	21.4	11.3	
263	273	227	125	29.6	30.7	25.6	14.1	

L: low psychological distress (10-15), M: moderate psychological distress (16-21), H: high psychological distress (22-29), VH: very high psychological distress (30-50).

Table 3 summarizes each case, as measured by the K10 scale, for low psychological distress (10–15), moderate psychological distress (16–21), high psychological distress (22–29), and very high psychological distress (30–50), on the basis of sex and age distribution. Figure 1 shows the distribution of scores for the K10 scale by high (19–30) and non-high (6–18) psychological distress group, with the K6 scale (i.e., sum of the response scores can range from 6 to 30). The very high psychological distress group (30–50) on the K10 scale is approximately compatible with the high psychological distress group (19–30) on the K6 scale.

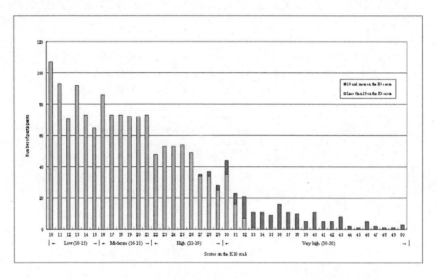

Figure 1. Distribution of scores on the Kessler 10 scale by two groups of Kessler 6 scale (<19 or ≥19).

Table 4 distinguishes employees with high or very high psychological distress (22–50) from the others (10–21), and presents information pertaining to the number and percentages of the high or very high K10 scores group by the socio-demographic status and employment-related variables of each category. The overall prevalence of high or very high psychological distress was 37.2% (33.7% for males, 39.6% for females). The prevalence of high or very high psychological distress among males was found to be higher than that among females in the age groups of 30–39 years and 40–49 years. Conversely, it was found to be lower than that of females in the age group of 29 years or younger, and 50 years and older. Further, a lower prevalence of high psychological distress was observed among females in the older age groups, unlike the equivalent age groups in the males.

Table 4. Demographics of samples according to the category of high or very high psychological distress based on the Kessler 10 (K10) scores and the differences between high or very high psychological distress group and the others

	Overall		Male		Female	
	H/VH	% H/VH	H/VH	% H/VH	H/VH	% H/VH
Sex *	562	(37.2)	210	(33.7)	352	(39.6)
Age **						
-29	140	(42.2)	38	(33.0)	102	(47.0)
30-39	169	(41.1)	63	(41.4)	106	(40.9)
40-49	146	(37.0)	57	(37.7)	89	(36.5)
50-	107	(28.6)	52	(25.2)	55	(32.7)
Education *						
Compulsory/senior high school	242	(34.6)	148	(34.7)	94	(34.4)
Tertiary education	286	(41.1)	45	(35.7)	241	(42.3)
Graduate degree or higher	30	(30.9)	16	(26.2)	14	(38.9)
Unknown	4	(20.0)	1	(9.1)	3	(33.3)
Employment status						
Full-time work	497	(37.0)	187	(33.3)	310	(39.7)
Part-time work	59	(37.3)	21	(36.2)	38	(38.0)
Unknown	6	(50.0)	2	(50.0)	4	(50.0)
Employee type						
Managerial class	52	(32.3)	30	(27.3)	22	(43.1)
Non-managerial class	504	(37.9)	180	(35.2)	324	(39.6)
Unknown	6	(27.3)	0	(0.0)	6	(31.6)
Job category **						
Clerical/administrative	51	(25.0)	27	(24.8)	24	(25.3)
Sales/service	70	(40.9)	34	(34.0)	36	(50.7)
Professional/technical	317	(41.0)	84	(39.4)	233	(41.6)
Others (on-site workers, etc.)	107	(34.1)	59	(33.3)	48	(35.0)
Unknown	17	(34.0)	6	(24.0)	11	(44.0)
Working hours per day						
8 hours or less	291	(35.7)	82	(32.2)	209	(37.4)
More than 8 hours	267	(38.9)	127	(34.7)	140	(43.6)
Unknown	4	(36.4)	1	(33.3)	3	(37.5)

H/VH: high or very high psychological distress (a value of 22-50 on the K10 scale). Significances representing the differences between high or very high psychological distress group and the others about the total number of cases for each category (Pearson's χ^2 statistic). $p< 0.05$, ** $p< 0.001$.

The results of Pearson's χ^2 test showed significant differences between the high or very high psychological distress group and the others, with regard to sex ($p < 0.05$), age distribution ($p < 0.001$), education ($p < 0.05$), and job category ($p < 0.001$). Furthermore, higher percentages of high or very high K10 scores were obtained for females compared to males in terms of employment status (full-time work and part-time work), employee type (managerial class and non-managerial class), job category (all sub-categories), and working hours per day (8 hours or less, and more than 8 hours).

Table 5. Correlation between the locus of control (LOC) scale and the Kessler 10 (K10) scale by sex and age distribution (Spearman's rank correlation)

	Overall	Male	Female
Age	r_s	r_s	r_s
-29	-0.366 *	-0.281 *	-0.427 *
30-39	-0.302 *	-0.378 *	-0.257 *
40-49	-0.304 *	-0.334 *	-0.277 *
50-	-0.302 *	-0.344 *	-0.243 *
Total	-0.311 *	-0.333 *	-0.290 *

r_s: Spearman's rank correlation coefficient * $p < 0.01$.

Table 6. Effects of socio-demographic status, employment-related variables, and locus of control scale on the Kessler 10 (K10) psychological distress scale (stepwise multiple regression analysis)

	Extracted factors	B	β
Overall	Age (50-)	-2.221	-0.119 *
($R^2 = 0.149$)	Job category (Clerical/administrative)	-1.725	-0.074 *
	Locus of control scale	-0.412	-0.349 *
Male	Age (50-)	-2.530	-0.145 *
($R^2 = 0.163$)	Locus of control scale	-0.416	-0.374 *
Female	Education (Compulsory/senior high school)	-2.224	-0.130 *
($R^2 = 0.132$)	Locus of control scale	-0.416	-0.337 *

R^2: coefficient of determinant; B, regression coefficient; β, standardized regression coefficient. * $p < 0.01$.

Table 5 presents the correlation between the K10 scales and the LOC scale sub-divided by sex and age distributions. Both the males and females in all age groups showed significantly negative correlations ($p < 0.01$; Spearman's rank correlation). Figure 2 shows the distribution of scores for the LOC scale by sex. Table 6 presents the effects of socio-demographic status, employment-related factors, and the LOC scale on the K10 psychological distress scale, using multiple regression analyses. Unstandardized (B) and standardized (β) regression coefficients are provided. The analysis of the effects of socio-demographic status, employment-related variables, and the LOC scale on the K10 scale indicates that the independent effects of age (50 years and older), job category (clerical/administrative), and the LOC scale on the K10 scale were significant for all participants ($p < 0.01$). Furthermore, age (50 years and older) and the LOC scale were significant for males ($p < 0.01$). Conversely, for females, education (compulsory/senior high school) and the LOC scale were significant ($p < 0.01$).

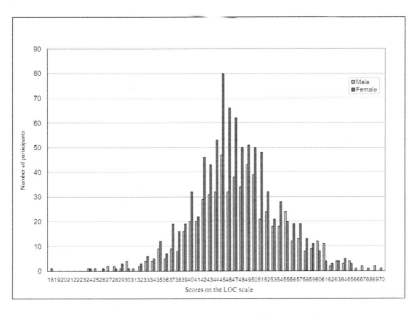

Figure 2. Distribution of scores on the locus of control (LOC) scale.

COMPARATIVE STUDIES ON THE RESULTS

The response rate of 87.3% for this survey is much higher than the typical response rate obtained in the case of employee-administered health questionnaires in many large organizations [7, 8, 18–20]. In spite of excluding responses with insufficient data, the response rate for this survey would still be considered high when compared to response rates obtained from population epidemiological studies.

In the present study, as many as 37.2% of the employees exhibited high (23.6%) or very high (13.6%) levels of psychological distress. Another study conducted in Australia estimated the risk of high or very high levels of psychological distress on the K10 psychological distress scale among the general population as 10.6%, and among "employed persons" (as a sub-group) as 8.4% [14]. The 37.2% prevalence rate of high or very high psychological distress among employees noted in this study is clearly much higher than the prevalence rate estimated among the general population of Australia. Certain assumptions can be made based on these findings. Firstly, Japan's suicide rate increased considerably during the 1990s, which might have been the result of drastic social changes, such as the nation-wide economic crisis and the termination of the lifetime employment practice at many major companies [6, 8, 21–23]. Therefore, the reason for a higher prevalence rate of psychological distress may be partly explained by rapid changes for the worse in the economic and work environment [8]. Secondly, we believe the lack of an interviewer in the current study has resulted in more realistic reporting compared to that obtained from complex interviewer-administered surveys. The higher prevalence of psychological distress among our sample population may thus be partly explained by this methodological factor [7, 8, 13]. Thirdly, we suggest that a culturally different response style to questions relating to emotion is also connected to higher scores on the psychological distress scale. For instance, compared to the Chinese-Americans, the Japanese are reluctant to express their emotions openly in cases of positive affections; instead, they tend to show an intermediate response [24–29].

In this study, age group was a demographic variable that was significantly associated with psychological distress. Regarding the levels of K10 psychological distress scale by age distribution, another study in Australia identified that the percentages of high or very high K10 psychological distress scale were 11.1% in the age group 16–24 years, 13.3% in the age group 25–34 years, 9.9% in the age group 35–44 years, 11.5% in the age group 45–54 years, 10.7% in the age group 55–64 years, 8.2% in the age group 65–74 years, and 7.0% in the age group 75 years and over [14]. These results approximate the trend discovered in the present study, namely that the younger age groups were at a relatively high risk of psychological distress compared to the older age groups. Other studies conducted in the past reveal that depression is most commonly reported among younger respondents, particularly females [30–35]. The results of our study also supported these findings.

Furthermore, the level of education has also been significantly associated with psychological distress. Another study in Australia calculated the percentages of high or very high K10 psychological distress scale as 12.1% for "Incomplete high school", 10.1% for "Completed high school", 10.1% for "Trade Certificate/Diploma", 8.5% for "Bachelor's degree or higher", and 18.1% for "Other" [14]. This trend is approximately compatible with that uncovered in the present study for males. It is widely accepted that the prevalence of mental health problems increases with lower levels of educational attainment [1, 2, 8, 36, 37]. However, the results of previous studies are inconsistent in terms of the relationship between psychological distress and the level of educational attainment. For example, although the highest prevalence rates of psychological distress were noted among employees with the lowest level of formal education in certain studies, yet others have noted significantly high levels of psychological distress among employees with a postgraduate degree [38]. In this study, males with high levels of educational attainment (graduate degree or higher), have a low percentage of high or very high K10 scores, whereas females with high levels of educational attainment do not clearly show such a trend. The reason for this is unclear; however, we believe this may be so given that in Japan, compared to males, females are at a disadvantage with regard to whether their educational background adequately reflects their employee designation in later life [8]. Further studies are needed to verify this point.

In this study, job category was found to be significantly associated with the prevalence rates of high or very high psychological distress. The findings of the present study show that females in sales/service roles, and males in professional/technical roles exhibit the highest percentage of high or very high K10 scores (as seen in Table 4). With regard to the job category, other studies have reported that the highest prevalence of psychological distress was observed among females in operator and/or laborer roles, and among males in clerical and/or administrative roles [38, 39]. Moreover, on an average, across males and females, the highest prevalence rates for psychological distress were observed among individuals in sales-related positions; on the other hand, the lowest rates were observed among executives or senior managers [38, 39]. In brief, there is no consistent evidence of the relationship between job category and psychological distress in the literature, evidently because of the complexity of their relationship [8].

The LOC was hypothesized to moderate stressor-strain relations because it appears as the factor most likely to affect the coping styles of individuals. Comparatively little research has been conducted on how coping styles interact with psychological distress in an applied setting, although factors related to coping styles (such as the LOC) have a lengthy tradition of research [13]. Therefore, it is worthwhile to give some consideration to the effects that related socio-demographic and occupational factors may have on these variables. On observing the direct correlations between the LOC and the K10 scale (Spearman's rank correlation), a uniform pattern of findings emerged— all the significant correlations were negative, indicating that as the LOC score increased (greater internality), the K10 score decreased (less psychological distress). These results are in accordance with those observed in earlier research on psychological distress from job-related stressors, such as job demands [13, 40, 41]. For instance, externals are likely to undergo greater psychological distress than others. In contrast, internals are likely to undergo less psychological distress, even when the number of stressors is relatively larger [10, 13, 42].

A limitation of this study was cross-sectional sampling, which made it difficult to infer causality. The data sample was selected at random; however, the decision to participate in the project and respond to the survey was left entirely to the employers and employees respectively. Consequently, the current paper presents results based on a realistic approach. In particular, self-selection biases in the current data are representative of those inherent in any employee health assessment survey, unlike large epidemiological surveys based on general population probability samples [7, 8, 13].

The assessment of individual personality traits regarding internality-externality (LOC scale) is another limitation of this study, since it was based on a single questionnaire measurement. As previously noted, one reason for studying long-term coping styles is that not all coping are synchronous with stressful incidents or episodes; psychological distress builds up over months or years rather than being the response to a single stressful incident. One approach to investigating the long-term patterns of coping styles is to measure the coping behavior repeatedly. However, in this type of research design, the response obtained may in part be an artifact of the method utilized by repeatedly focusing the participants' attention on how they cope in the long term [12]. An alternative to this approach, which reduces the occurrence of such problems, is to examine the long-term patterns of coping styles, because the necessity of performing frequent repeated measures is reduced [12, 13].

CONCLUSION

The K10 is one of the most widely used psychological distress scales worldwide. Therefore, it should ideally be included in the health risk assessment of employees. This study revealed that 37.2% of the employees had high or very high K10 scores; indeed, higher prevalence of psychological distress was observed in this study than in previous studies. The prevalence rates presented in this paper may contribute to a set of reference values (or benchmarks) for employee psychological distress, thereby potentially enhancing the significance of future employment-based studies and corporate health risk appraisal surveys. The elucidation of the employee risk factors for psychological distress may improve mental health clinicians' understanding of employees, guide mental health prevention programs, and inform OSH departments about specific high-risk areas that should be targeted by mental health programs. In addition, this information will be useful to clinicians in order to increase awareness about the specific occupational risk factors that may help in predicting/diagnosing mental disorders.

ACKNOWLEDGMENTS

The author would like to thank Tetsuo Shimizu, Katsuyuki Murata, Yasutsugu Kudo, Masayuki Seki, Seiji Saito, and the staff of the Akita Occupational Health Promotion Center for their valuable comments and suggestions.

REFERENCES

[1]   Andrews G, Henderson S, Hall W: Prevalence, comorbidity, disability and service utilisation. Overview of the Australian National Mental Health Survey. *Br. J. Psychiatry* 2001; 178: 145–153.

[2]   Bijl RV, Ravelli A, van Zessen G: Prevalence of psychiatric disorder in the general population: results of The Netherlands Mental Health Survey and Incidence Study (NEMESIS). *Soc. Psychiatry Psychiatr. Epidemiol.* 1998; 33: 587–595.

[3] Bijl RV, de Graaf R, Hiripi E, Kessler RC, Kohn R, Offord DR, et al: The prevalence of treated and untreated mental disorders in five countries. *Health Aff.* 2003; 22: 122–133.

[4] Kessler RC, Chiu WT, Demler O, Merikangas KR, Walters EE: Prevalence, severity, and comorbidity of 12-month DSM-IV disorders in the National Comorbidity Survey Replication. *Arch. Gen. Psychiatry* 2005; 62: 617–627.

[5] Wells JE, Oakley Browne MA, Scott KM, McGee MA, Baxter J, Kokaua J: Te Rau Hinengaro: the New Zealand Mental Health Survey: overview of methods and findings. *Aust. N. Z. J. Psychiatry* 2006; 40: 835–844.

[6] Fushimi M, Sugawara J, Shimizu T: Suicide patterns and characteristics in Akita, Japan. *Psychiatry Clin. Neurosci.* 2005; 59: 296–302.

[7] Fushimi M, Shimizu T, Saito S, Kudo Y, Seki M, Murata K: Prevalence of and risk factors for psychological distress among employees in Japan. *Public Health* 2010; 124: 713–715.

[8] Fushimi M, Saito S, Shimizu T, Kudo Y, Seki M, Murata K: Prevalence of psychological distress, as measured by the Kessler 6 (K6), and related factors in Japanese employees. *Community Ment. Health J.* 2011 (in Press).

[9] Kessler RC, Barker PR, Colpe LJ, Epstein JF, Gfroerer JC, Hiripi E, Howes MJ, Normand SL, Manderscheid RW, Walters EE, Zaslavsky AM: Screening for serious mental illness in the general population. *Arch. Gen. Psychiatry* 2003; 60: 184–189.

[10] Rotter JB: Generalized expectancies for internal versus external control of reinforcement. *Psychol. Monographs* 1966; 80: 1–28.

[11] Parkes KR: Stressful episodes reported by first-year student nurses: a descriptive account. *Soc. Sci. Med.* 1985; 20: 945–953.

[12] Newton TJ, Keenan A: The moderating effect of the type A behavior pattern and locus of control upon the relationship between change in job demands and change in psychological strain. *Hum. Relat.* 1990; 43: 1229–1255.

[13] Fushimi M: The relationship between individual personality traits (internality-externality) and psychological distress in employees on Japan. *Depress. Res. Treat.* 2011 (in Press).

[14] Avery J, Dal Grande E, Taylor A, Gill T: Which South Australians experience psychological distress?: Kessler psychological distress 10-item scale July 2002-June 2004, *South Australian Monitoring and Surveillance System* (SAMSS), Population Research and Outcome

Studies Unit, 2004. http://www.sapo.org.au/pub/pub1604.html (http://health.adelaide.edu.au/pros/docs/reports/report2004_2007_samms_psyc hdistress.pdf).

[15] Baillie AJ: Predictive gender and education bias in Kessler's psychological distress Scale (k10). *Soc. Psychiatry Psychiatr. Epidemiol.* 2005; 40:743–748.

[16] Kambara M, Higuchi K, Shimizu N: Locus of control scale. In: H. Hori and Y. Yamamoto (Eds), *Book of psychometric scales* Vol. 1, pp. 180–184, Saiensu-sha, Tokyo, Japan, 2001 (in Japanese).

[17] Sasaki H, Kanachi M: The effects of trial repetition and individual characteristics on decision making under uncertainty. *J. Psychol.* 2005; 139: 233–246.

[18] Furukawa TA, Kessler RC, Slade T, Andrews G: The performance of the K6 and K10 screening scales for psychological distress in the Australian National Survey of Mental Health and Well-Being. *Psychol. Med.* 2003; 33: 357–362.

[19] Wang PS, Beck AL, McKenas DK, Meneades LM, Pronk NP, Saylor JS, et al: Effects of efforts to increase response rates on a workplace chronic condition screening survey. *Med. Care* 2002; 40: 752–760.

[20] Wang PS, Simon GE, Avorn J, Azocar F, Ludman EJ, McCulloch J, et al: Telephone screening, outreach, and care management for depressed workers and impact on clinical and work productivity outcomes: a randomized controlled trial. *JAMA* 2007; 298: 1401–1411.

[21] Fushimi M, Sugawara J, Shimizu T: Suicide in Akita Prefecture, Japan. *International Psychiatry* 2006; 3: 3–5.

[22] Fushimi M: Suicide Trends and Prevention in Akita Prefecture, Japan. *Quarterly Journal of Mental Health* 2007; 1: 51–55.

[23] Kishi Y, Kathol RG: Assessment of patients who attempt Suicide. *Prim. Care Companion J. Clin. Psychiatry* 2002; 4: 132–136.

[24] Cho MJ, Kim KH: Use of the Center for Epidemiologic Studies Depression Scale in Korea. *J. Nerv. Ment. Dis.* 1998; 186: 304–310.

[25] Cho MJ, Nam JJ, Suh GH: Prevalence of symptoms of depression in a nationwide sample of Korean adults. *Psychiatry Res.* 1998; 81: 341–352.

[26] Iwata N, Okuyama Y, Kawakami Y, Saito K: Prevalence of depressive symptoms in a Japanese occupational setting: a preliminary study. *Am. J. Public Health* 1989; 79: 1486–1489.

[27] Iwata N, Saito K, Roberts RE: Responses to a self-administered depression scale among younger adolescents in Japan. *Psychiatry Res.* 1994; 53: 275–287.

[28] Rankin SH, Galbraith ME: Reliability and validity data for a Chinese translation for the CES-D. *Psychol. Rep.* 1993; 73:1291–1298.

[29] Iwata N, Umesue M, Egashira K, Hiro H, Mizoue T, Mishima N et al: Can positive affect items be used to assess depressive disorders in the Japanese population? *Psychol. Med.* 1998; 28: 153–158.

[30] Comstock GW, Helsing KJ: Symptoms of depression in two communities. *Psychol. Med.* 1976; 6: 551–563.

[31] Craig TJ, Van Natta PA: Influence of demographic characteristics on two measures of depressive symptoms: the relation of prevalence and persistence of symptoms with sex, age, education, and marital status. *Arch. Gen. Psychiatry* 1979; 36: 149–154.

[32] Husaini BA, Neff JA, Harrington JB, Houghs MD, Stone RH: Depression in rural communities: validating the CES-D scale. *J. Community Psychol.* 1980; 8: 20–27.

[33] Madianos MG, Tomaras V, Kapsali A, Vaidakis N, Vlachonicolis J, Stefanis CN: Psychiatric case identification in two Athenian communities: estimation of the probable prevalence. *Acta Psychiatr. Scand.* 1988; 78:24–31.

[34] Narrow WE, Rae DS, Moscicki EK, Locke BZ, Regier DA: Depression among Cuban Americans: the Hispanic Health and Nutrition Examination Survey. *Soc. Psychiatry Psychiatr. Epidemiol.* 1990; 25: 260–268.

[35] Radloff LS: The CES-D scale: a report of depression scale for research in the general population. *Appl. Psychol. Meas.* 1977; 1: 385–401.

[36] Pratt LA, Dey AN, Cohen AJ: *Characteristics of adults with serious psychological distress as measured by the K6 scale:* United States, 2001-04. Adv Data 2007; 1–18.

[37] Stewart WF, Ricci JA, Chee E, Hahn SR, Morganstein D: Cost of lost productive work time among US workers with depression. *JAMA* 2003; 289: 3135–3144.

[38] Hilton MF, Whiteford HA, Sheridan JS, Cleary CM, Chant DC, Wang PS, et al: The prevalence of psychological distress in employees and associated occupational risk factors. *J. Occup. Environ. Med.* 2008; 50: 746–757.

[39] Kessler RC, Frank RG: The impact of psychiatric disorders on work loss days. *Psychol. Med.* 1997; 27: 861–873.

[40] Keenan A, McBain GDM: Effects of type A behaviour, intolerance of ambiguity, and locus of control on the relationship between role stress and work-related outcomes. *J. Occup. Psychol.* 1979; 52: 277–285.

[41] Jackson SE, Schuler RS: A meta-analysis and conceptual critique of research on role ambiguity and role conflict in work settings. *Organ Behav. Hum. Decision Processes* 1985; 36: 16–78.

[42] Rotter JB: Some problems and misconceptions related to the construct of internal versus external control of reinforcement. *J. Consult. Clin. Psychol.* 1975; 43: 56–67.

In: Psychological Distress   ISBN: 978-1-61942-646-7
Editors: H. Ohayashi and S. Yamada   © 2012 Nova Science Publishers, Inc.

Chapter 6

PSYCHOLOGICAL DISTRESS IN THE MILITARY AND MINDFULNESS BASED TRAINING

Melba C. Stetz,[1,], Heather H. McDermott,[1]*
Michael R. Brumage,[2] Philip A. Holcombe,
Raymond A. Folen,[1] and Ivana Steigman[3]
[1]Tripler Army Medical Center, Honolulu, HI, US
[2]Schofield Barracks Health Clinic, Schofield Barracks, Honolulu, HI, US
[3]Thrive Research, Inc., Los Altos, CA, US

ABSTRACT

Objective: Service members and their dependents represent a group who have been experiencing an increased amount of stress due to events such as multiple deployments and exposure to combat. As stress levels in the military rise and warfighters return from theater with complex psychological presentations, the need for evidence-based practices aimed at stress reduction becomes increasingly necessary. Mindfulness meditation is an evidence-based intervention that encourages individuals to bring their awareness to the present moment. Such practice can deliver

* The views expressed in this article are those of the authors and do not necessarily represent the
official policy or position of the Department of Defense or the U.S. Army Medical Command.
Contact: Lieutenant Colonel Melba C. Stetz. Email: melba.stetz@us.army.mil. Guarantor:
Major Melba C. Stetz.

104   M. C. Stetz, H. H. McDermott, M. R. Brumage et al.

the benefits of decreasing stress and pain and increasing emotional
regulation. This manuscript explores the opinions of civilian and military
providers working with the military population and their attitudes towards
the utility of mindfulness-based practices for the military. The results
from a two-day Mindfulness Workshop in Honolulu, Hawaii are
highlighted. Insight into providers attitudes towards Mindfulness
techniques may inform possible future applications for Mindfulness
based interventions as well as future trainings. Methods: An anonymous
self-survey titled Mindfulness Workshop Follow-up Questionnaire 1
(Post-Training) was administered to capture attending providers
satisfaction with the Mindfulness training workshop. Results: 111 civilian
and military providers responded to the questionnaire. Findings suggested
that providers living in Hawaii were experiencing a high level of stress 7
(measured on Likert scale of 0-10 with 0 being no stress and 10 being
extremely stressful). Attendees identified their superiors as being the
group most in need of taking the Mindfulness training (79%). A large
percentage of providers anticipated using this training in their personal
lives (74%). Conclusions: Results of the survey confirm the body of
literature cited that purposes a high level of stress present among the
military population. Providers rated Mindfulness based trainings as being
a promising tool to be used in a military setting as well as in their
personal lives.

Keywords: mindfulness, military stress, military families

"Dum loquimur, fugerit invida Aetas: carpe diem, quam minimum
credula postero."
In English: "While we're talking, envious time is fleeing: seize the day,
put no trust in the future." Horace

INTRODUCTION

Stress can be defined as "a physical, chemical, or emotional factor that
causes bodily or mental tension and that may be a factor in disease causation"
(Merriam-Webster, 2001). The American Stress Institute states that it is hard
to define psychological stress since it is a subjective sensation that can be
perceived and conceptualized differently from person to person (Rosch, 2009).
Furthermore, stress can play different roles as that of a cause ("stressor") or
effect ("strain"). Therefore, psychologists spend a significant amount of time
testing different modalities to help their patients suffering from stress and
anxiety. Due to the complexity of behavioral health problems (e.g.,

Posttraumatic Stress Disorder) complementary therapeutic or training approaches are proving to be useful.

Service members and their dependents represent a particular group who have been experiencing an increased amount of stress due to such events as multiple deployments and exposure to combat. As stress levels in the military rise and warfighters return from theater with complex psychological presentations, the need for evidence-based practices aimed at stress reduction becomes increasingly necessary. Mindfulness meditation is an evidence-based technique that encourages individuals to bring their awareness to the present moment. Such practice can deliver benefits of decreasing stress and pain and increasing emotional regulation. This manuscript explores the opinions of civilian and military providers working with the military population and their attitudes towards the utility of mindfulness-based practices. The results from a two-day Mindfulness Workshop in Honolulu, Hawaii are highlighted. Insight into providers' attitudes towards Mindfulness techniques may inform possible future applications for Mindfulness based trainings in the military.

STRESS IN THE UNITED STATES

The American Psychological Association (2007) administered a stress survey to 1,848 individuals. Results suggested that one-third of US citizens are living with extreme stress. Money was indicated as one of the main stressors for about three quarters of this sample. Many participants in this study also reported experiencing psychological symptoms of stress including irritability or anger (50 %); feeling nervous (45 %); lack of energy (45 %); and feeling ready to cry (35 %). Almost half (48 %) of the sample reported lying awake at night due to their stress. The participants' main somatic stress symptoms reported were: fatigue (51 %); headache (44 %); upset stomach (34 %); muscle tension (30 %); change in appetite (23 %), teeth grinding (17 %); change in sex drive (15 %); and feeling dizzy (13 %) (APA, 2007).

STRESS IN THE US MILITARY

Due to the unique culture and persistent high wartime operational tempo, service in the United States military may be stressful for service members and families as well as for those who care for both groups. The frequent moves, prolonged family separation (e.g., deployments) and reintegration can significantly stress the individual as well as the family homeostasis. Furthermore, many service members and families enter into a military lifestyle without the tools to successfully navigate through it.

Hoge, Auchterloni, and Milliken (2006) suggest that 1 out of 10 U.S. Operation Iraqi Freedom (OIF) veterans typically suffer from some type of stress disorder. Similarly, Huffman, Culbertson, & Castro (2008) cite a study indentifying the type of care veterans receive from operations overseas (e.g., OIF; n = 103,788). This study suggested that about 1/3 of those that received care from 2001 to 2005 were either diagnosed with mental health or psycho-social problems. In fact, PTSD was the most common disorder diagnosed. 13,205 veterans received a PTSD diagnosis, which accounted for more than half (52 %) of the mental health diagnoses. Other disorders included anxiety disorder (24 %), adjustment disorder (24%), depression (20 %), and substance abuse (20 %). Furthermore, of those that sought VA services, 13% were due to PTSD, which is less than the15 % for veterans from the Vietnam War, but more than the 3.5 % reported in the general population.

Chronic psychological and physiological symptoms of distress negatively impact warfighters' operational performance and increase vulnerability in the war-zone. The stress incurred from deployments has the capacity to reach beyond service members themselves. The warfighters' family system can also be subjected to various degrees of stress and emotional suffering is incurred from separation due to a mandatory deployment. A soldier's declining emotional health, physical absence, and lack of communication often perpetuates a cycle where the warfighter feels incapable to help his/her family while protecting his country. Furthermore, upon returning home, the warfighter may add to the stress from combat when he or she might to struggle with reintegration as well as possible change in family dynamics (Huffman, Culbertson, & Castro, 2008).

The balance of work and family presents "unique stressors" for service members and their families such as, "adjustment to a mobile lifestyle, isolation from the civilian community and extended family, adjustment to the rules and regulations of military life, and frequent family separations" (Eaton, Messer, Castro, & Hoge, 2005, n.p.). Moreover, the rates of generalized anxiety disorder among military spouses have found to be similar to those found in service members. Military stressors and social stressors such as those described above, can lead service members returning from war to develop psychological problems such as Anxiety Disorders or exacerbate Post-Traumatic Stress Disorder (PTSD) symptoms. In addition, such stressors may contribute to the potential presence of co-morbid disorders such substance abuse or depression.

Consequently, clinicians must often address marriage and family problems in addition to psychological and physiological complaints from service members. Most of the typical providers' effort has been on diagnosing and treating high risk service members and their families. However, new efforts are being made to utilize techniques that also prevent family stress and that promote resilience and post-traumatic growth (Agee, Danoff-Burg, Grant, 2009). As illustrated earlier, the rate of stress in the United States is high among both a military and a civilian population. In addition, the rates of disorders like anxiety and PTSD are on the rise. For psychologists working in the public service, especially among a military population, incorporating stress-reduction interventions into treatment may prove to be especially useful.

MINDFULNESS TRAINING

Agee, Danoff-Burg, & Grant (2009) assert that the concept of *Mindfulness* may be viewed as "an intentional awareness of our present-moment experience in a direct and accepting way" (p.104). Carmody & Baer (2009) highlight that in mindfulness training, participants are taught the practice of abandoning "goals" and "expectations" in order to accept mental representations at face value (p. 627). Irving, Dobkin, Park (2009) suggest that mindfulness training teaches us to achieve "self-regulation" of our mind's desire to "distract our attention from the real demands of our situation" (p. 66). Shapiro, Astin, Bishop, & Cordova (2005) recognize that mindfulness practices seek to foster awareness that is "non-judgmental and "purposeful" (p. 65). Such practices can be associated with other relaxation and (maybe ironically) concentration practices such as transcendental or object focused meditation. Thus, rather than encouraging participants to sustain a "focus upon any specific object or mantra," mindfulness distinguishes itself in that it encourages its participants to allow a "state of fluid attention" to develop (Shapiro et al., 2005, p. 165). Consequently, they assert it is appropriate to view mindfulness as an entity separate from other meditation practices.

MINDFULNESS RESEARCH

Mindfulness-based stress reduction (MBSR) may be viewed as a standardized treatment modality used to treat complaints like stress, anxiety, and depression (Kang, Choi, & Ryu, 2009). Kabat-Zinn designed the original MBSR program with a psycho-educational curriculum that ran for 8 weeks. During this time attendees were exposed to a variety of meditation practices, which they were required to practice in their daily lives. The rationale was that through the continued use of meditation practices, stress would be alleviated over time (Grossman, Niemann, Schmidt, & Walach, 2004).

Research focused on clinical populations shows that MBSR has the ability to reduce stress related to a variety of complaints such as chronic pain, generalized anxiety, and other psychiatric disorders (Pace, Negi, Adame, et al, 2009). Studies also suggest that the application of MBSR to health care professionals, a population noted for its high stress and burnout rates, is effective in stress reduction (Grossman, P., Niemann, L., Schmidt, S., & Walach, H. 2004,). Other promising applications include implementing MBSR in treatment plans for individuals with Irritable Bowel Syndrome (IBS)(Kearney, & Brown-Chang, 2008). MBSR may also be used in conjunction with complementary therapies such as progressive muscle relaxation. With the high rate of PTSD among our warfighter population, such stress reduction treatment modalities such as MBSR may be especially appropriate. However, there is a dearth of current literature on the effectiveness of MBSR on this population.

MINDFULNESS TRAINING FOR
PROVIDER RESIDING IN HAWAII

A popular assumption held by many is that residents of Hawaii do not experience as much stress as their mainland counterparts because they live in a vacation destination. However, Hawaii residents are not immune to commonplace stressors such as balancing work and personal life obstacles, unemployment, and relational issues. In fact, the cost of living in Hawaii is well above the national average in the areas of home prices, health care, property taxes, insurance, and education (Cost of Living by State, 2009).

Military personnel and their dependents represent sizable population among the residents of Hawaii. In Hawaii, military residents and their families who are experiencing stress are served by the Tripler Army Medical Center (TAMC), a tertiary care center, the Schofield Barracks Health Clinic, and the Naval Medical Clinic, Pearl Harbor. These facilities, all located on the island of Oahu, provide services related to behavioral health issues. The TAMC is the headquarters of the Pacific Regional Medical Command, a command that serves deployed forces in more than 40 countries and territories. TAMC sponsored a two-day workshop held in Honolulu, Hawaii, in order to introduce providers to stress-reduction Mindfulness Training. Two Mindfulness trainers from the University of Massachusetts Mindfulness Center and Georgetown University were invited to conduct this Mindfulness Workshop.

METHODS

Participants

The information presented in this manuscript is based on the attitudes of civilian (n = 81; 76%) and military providers, working with the military, who attended a two-day Mindfulness Workshop in Hawaii. The total number of respondents was 111. Most of them were females (n = 62, 78 %). Most of the respondents were between the ages of 22 and 44 years (n = 55, 54%).

Measures

To measure the perceived usefulness and potential use of Mindfulness training for a military population, Stetz and the instructors developed an anonymous self-survey titled "Mindfulness Workshop Follow-up Questionnaire 1 (Post-Training)." This survey was developed to capture respondents' satisfaction with the Mindfulness training workshop and the potential for future use of the skills that they acquired. The survey consisted of a few demographic questions (e.g., gender) and a question to rate their level of stress in life (see Figure 1, "1" = "no stress" and "10" = "extremely stressful"). In addition, this survey included 3 scales that measured the perceived utility of mindfulness training in the military. Specifically, these questions were designed to cover: "Overall Training" (6 questions), "Training Content" (7 questions), and "Future Use" (6 questions), with a scale ranging from"1" = "Strongly Disagree" to "5" = "Strongly Agree."

RESULTS

The three scales of the Mindfulness Workshop Follow-up Questionnaire 1 (Post-Training) were locally created. However, their reliability estimates were fairly high. Specifically, Overall Training (OT, 6 items) yielded a Cronbach Alpha (α) of 0.96. The Training Content (TC, 7 items) yielded 0.96 and Future Training (FT, 6 items) yielded an α of 0.93.

As depicted in Table 1, the highest endorsed item in the OT scale was *"I would recommend that my superiors in the military take this introductory mindfulness TNG (79%)."* The lowest endorsed item was *"I would recommend that my family take this introductory mindfulness TNG (67%)."* In the TC, the highest one was *"I anticipate using these skills in my personal life (74%)"* while the lowest item was *"I anticipate using these skills in my professional life (during deployment, 44%)."* Finally, the highest item in the FU scale was *"I believe that if I made use of these practices, I would benefit from doing so (72%)"* and the lowest one was *"I anticipate practicing these exercises in the morning (38%).*

After comparing each of the scales and correlating these with the demographic variables (i.e. number, gender, age) and the Life Stress item, the only significant correlation was between OT and TC (r = 0.90, p = 0.00); OT and FU (r = 0.85, p = 0.00), and FU and TC was (r = 0.81, p = 0.00). There was no significant correlation between any of these three variables with the Life stress item.

As we can see in Figure 1, the highest ranked number in the Life Stress item for civilian attendees was 7, followed by 8 for the total sample. Highlighted by Figure 2, the opposite was true for the military attendees. That is, their highest rank score for was 8 followed by 7. That said, when further analyzing this data by membership (civilian vs. military) there was no statistical difference (t(104)= -.41, p=.69).

This was a one-time cross-sectional survey, which does not test actual training efficacy. Although this was intended to be an anonymous survey, future research should consider following their surveys in more than one time point for potential longitudinal prediction (e.g., continued use and efficacy of Mindfulness skills). A baseline or "Pre-workshop training test" would have also been useful to determine participants' views on Mindfulness prior to the workshop.

Each of the three scales seemed to be statistically reliable (all alphas higher than .90). Also, items' endorsement mainly suggested that respondents would recommend Mindfulness training to their superiors. In addition, they anticipated using the skills learned in the workshop in their personal lives. Finally, participants stated that if practicing these skills, they would benefit from it. All three scales in the survey were correlated. However, none of these correlated with the Life Stress item. That said, in accordance with the literature, the whole sample rated their life stress as high (7).

Table 1. Survey items and corresponding response rates

		Score (1 - 5)	
		Lowest n (%)	Highest n (%)
I	**Overall Training**		
1	"I enjoyed taking this introductory mindfulness TNG."	2 (1)	5 (72)
2	"I would recommend that my subordinates in the military take this introductory mindfulness TNG."	2 (2)	5 (69)
3	"I would recommend that my peers in the military take this introductory mindfulness TNG."	2 (2)	5 (74)
4	"I would recommend that my superiors in the military take this introductory mindfulness TNG. "	2 (2)	5 (79)
5	"I would recommend that my family take this introductory mindfulness TNG."	1 (3)	5 (67)
6	"I would recommend that my friends take this introductory mindfulness TNG."	2 (2)	5 (68)
II	**Training Content**		
1	"I learned a lot from this TNG."	2 (2)	5 (58)
2	"I learned valuable skills from this TNG."	2 (2)	5 (58)
3	"I learned about myself from this TNG."	1 (4); 2 (4)	5 (54)
4	"I anticipate using these skills in my personal life."	2 (2)	5 (74)
5	"I anticipate using these skills in my professional life (while in garrison)."	1 (3)	5 (55)
6	"I anticipate using these skills in my professional life (during deployment)."	1 (4)	5 (44)
7	"I anticipate using these skills with my patients."	2 (1)	5 (55)

Table 1. (Continued)

III	Future Use of Mindfulness Exercises		
1	"I anticipate practicing regularly after this TNG."	2 (3)	5 (49)
2	"I anticipate practicing during particularly stressful or traumatic experiences."	2 (2)	5 (61)
3	"I anticipate practicing these exercises in the morning."	1 (7)	5 (38)
4	"I anticipate practicing these exercises in the evening."	1 (4)	5 (41)
5	"I anticipate practicing these exercises while exercising."	1 (4)	5 (45)
6	"I believe that if I made use of these practices, I would benefit from doing so."	1 (4)	5 (72)

On a scale of 1 to 10, where 1 is no stress and 10 is extremely stressful, how stressful is your life right now?

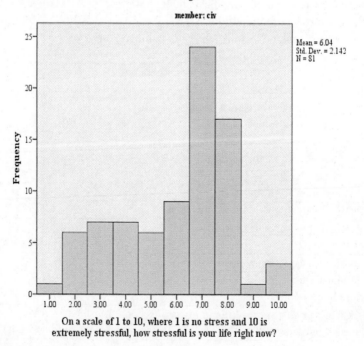

On a scale of 1 to 10, where 1 is no stress and 10 is extremely stressful, how stressful is your life right now?

Figure 1. Reported Stress Levels for Civilian Attendees.

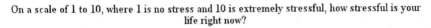

On a scale of 1 to 10, where 1 is no stress and 10 is extremely stressful, how stressful is your life right now?

member: mil

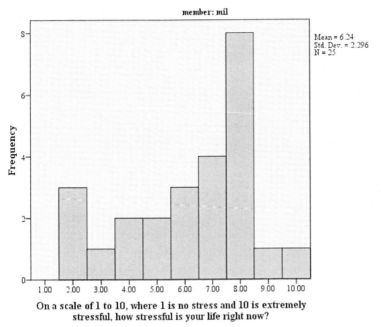

Mean = 6.24
Std. Dev. = 2.296
N = 25

On a scale of 1 to 10, where 1 is no stress and 10 is extremely stressful, how stressful is your life right now?

Figure 2. Reported Stress Levels for Military Attendees.

Specifically, of the total sample the highest number selected in the Life Stress item was 7, followed by 8. However, the opposite was true for the military sample. Even though there was no statistical significance between these differences, due to the combat casualty rates further studies should seek larger military samples to assist providers working in the military sector.

This cross-sectional survey represented a disproportionate number of civilian to military providers. It may be useful in the future to administer it again to a larger sample of military providers to gain a deeper understanding of the appropriateness of mindfulness training for providers working in a military setting. Also, although this was intended to be an anonymous survey, future workshops should consider following their surveys in more than one time point for potential longitudinal prediction (e.g., continued use and perceived usefulness of Mindfulness skills). A baseline or "Pre-workshop training test" would have also been useful to determine respondents' views on Mindfulness prior to the workshop. Nevertheless, results from our survey suggest that even the population residing or stationed in a "relaxing" environment such as the vacation destination of Hawaii may experience stress and benefit from Mindfulness.

CONCLUSION

Mindfulness training can be conceptualized as a reaction to the zeitgeist of our time which places little value in enjoying time in the moment. It can be perceived as a method aimed at focusing oneself on the present moment. As service members and their families continue to experience psychological distress and the military system keeps searching for a better way to ameliorate such stress, mindfulness training may be considered a useful intervention.

In examining the descriptive results from the survey, several points of interest emerged in the descriptive analysis. Among the military population, the recommendation that superiors take the mindfulness training workshop was made. In addition, the recommendation that military peers take the workshop received another large rate of response. Participants indicated that they did not anticipate using the skills in their professional lives as much as their personal lives. This finding deserves further exploration as the research cited in this paper suggests that military families experience stress levels similar to those of warfighters.

One of the more apparent findings of the survey was that military and civilian participants both rate their stress level as being extremely high. As table 1 suggests, most participants rank their level of current stress at the higher end of the continuum, with 7 and 8 being the most validated responses. Such a finding is consistent with statistics cited in this study for stress levels among both civilian and military populations.

The survey created describes not only the current stress levels of providers living in a vacation destination (i.e., Hawaii) and working with a military population, but also describes their opinions as to the utility of mindfulness training in their personal and professional lives. The sample described was diverse in that it used both civilian and military providers who represented various ages, military ranks, and both female and male genders. In comparison of the demographics represented by the survey, it is interesting to note that a much larger sample of females than males attended the training. Thus, further examination of whether a gender bias exists in Mindfulness training among providers is warranted. Also, identifying whether an age bias occurs in mindfulness training would be of interest as the largest group in the sample was over 45 years old and no participant was under the age of 21.

We also acknowledge some limitations with this survey administration. For example, this was a one-time cross-sectional survey, which does not test actual training efficacy. This survey should be administered again, at different points in time (e.g., three months after the training). In addition, a Pre-training test would have been useful to determine participants' views on Mindfulness prior to the workshop. Also, the low number of military attendees makes comparison between military and civilian participants difficult. Lastly, because this was a descriptive study, no causative statements could be made regarding the effect of Mindfulness training on participants' stress levels, or their attitudes towards the training itself.

As highlighted, military life can be stressful for service members, families, and providers, even in a "relaxing" environment such as the vacation destination of Hawaii. The findings in this study suggest that participants experienced high levels of stress. Furthermore, participants found utility in using Mindfulness training to help combat stress. Research exploring the application of mindfulness based practices are warranted. In addition, as this chapter identifies the high levels of stress occurring among military dependents, using mindfulness based practices may be appropriate and should be further explored.

REFERENCES

Agee, J., Danoff-Burg, S., Grant, C. (2009). Comparing brief stress management courses in a community sample: Mindfulness skills and progressive muscle relaxation. *Explore*, 5(2), 104-109.

Carmody, J, Baer, R. (2009). How long does a mindfulness-based stress reduction program need to be? A review of class contact hours and effect sizes for psychological distress. *Journal of Clinical Psychology*, 65(6), 627-638.

Cost of Living by State. Cost of living statistics by state. Available at: www.costoflivingbystate.org; accessed November 30, 2009.

Eaton, K. M, Messer, S. C., Castro, C. A., Hoge, C. W. Military spouse mental health outcomes and care utilization. Presented at the American Psychological Association, Conference, August 18-21 2005, Washington, District of Columbia.

Grossman, P., Niemann, L., Schmidt, S., & Walach, H. (2004). Mindfulness-based stress reduction and health benefits: A meta-analysis. *Journal of Psychosomatic Research*, 57, 35–43.

Hoge, C. W., Auchterloni, J. L., Milliken, C. S. (2006). Mental health problems, use of mental health services, and attrition from military service after returning from deployment to Iraq or Afghanistan. *The Journal of the American Medical Association, 295* (9), 1023-1032.

Huffman, A. H., Culbertson, S. S., Castro, C. A. (2008). Family-friendly environments and U.S. army soldier performance and work outcomes. *Military Psychology, 20*(4), 253-270.

Irving, J., Dobkin, P., Park, J. (2009). Cultivating mindfulness in health care professionals: A review of empirical studies of mindfulness-based stress reduction [MBSR]. *Complementary Therapies in Clinical Practice. 15*, 61-66.

Kang, Y. S., Choi, S. Y., Ryu, E. (2009). The Effectiveness of a stress coping program based on mindfulness meditation on the stress, anxiety, and depression experienced by nursing students in korea. *Nurse Education Today, 29*(5), 538-543.

Kearney D. J., Brown-Chang J. (2008). Complementary and alternative medicine for IBS in adults: Mind-body interventions. *Nature Clinic Practice Gastroenterol Hepatol, 5*(11): 624-636.

Merriam-Webster. (2001). Definition of stress. Retrieved from: http://www.merriam-webster.com/dictionary/stress.

Pace, T. W, Negi, L. T., Adame, D. D., Cole, S. P., Sivilli, T. I., Brown, T. D., Issa, M. J., Raison, C. L. (2009). Effect of compassion meditation on neuroendrocrine, innate immune and behavioral responses to psychosocial stress. *Psychoneuroendocrinology, 34*(1), 87-98.

Rosch, P. J. (2009). The American Institute of Stress: The role of health and stress in mental illness. Retrieved from: http://www.stress.org.

Shapiro S., Astin J., Bishop S., Cordova M. (2005). Mindfulness-based stress reduction for health care professionals: Results from a randomized trial. *International Journal of Stress Management, 12* (2):164-176.

The American Psychological Association. (2007). Stress survey. Retrieved from: http: //www. apa.org/releases/stressproblem.

Tripler Army Medical Center. About tamc. Available at: http://www.tamc.amedd.army.mil/information/about_tamc/aboutUs.htm; accessed November 30, 2009.

In: Psychological Distress ISBN: 978-1-61942-646-7
Editors: H. Ohayashi and S. Yamada © 2012 Nova Science Publishers, Inc.

Chapter 7

IMPACT OF PSYCHOLOGICAL DISTRESS IN INFERTILE JAPANESE WOMEN[*]

Hidehiko Matsubayashi[1,†] *Takashi Hosaka*[2]
and Tsunehisa Makino[1]
[1]Department of Obstetrics and Gynecology,
[2]Department of Psychiatry and Behavioral Science,
Tokai University School of Medicine, Bohseidai,
Isehara, Kanagawa, Japan

ABSTRACT

Infertile women in Japan as well as in the Western World have high
levels of emotional distress, which include anxiety and depression. By
cross-sectional questionnaire study, both scores of the hospital anxiety
and depression scale (HADS) and the profile of mood states (POMS) for
infertile Japanese women were high, indicating psychologically
disturbed. In Japan, women are frequently greeted with traditional
questions such as, 'Are you married? Do you have a child?' Elderly
Japanese may project guilt on women without children, because they

---

* A version of this chapter also appears in *Advances in Psychology Research, Volume 56*, edited
by Alexandra M. Columbus, published by Nova Science Publishers, Inc. It was submitted for
appropriate modifications in an effort to encourage wider dissemination of research.
†Correspondence: Hidehiko Matsubayashi M.D., Ph.D.; Department of Obstetrics and
Gynecology, Tokai University School of Medicine, Bohseidai, Isehara, Kanagawa, 259-1193
Japan. e-mail: hide-m@is.icc.u-tokai.ac.jp; FAX: 81+463-91-4343

believe women should fulfill a role by producing an heir and/or heiress to continue the family name. This can cast shame and/or guilt on the infertility patients, and thus produce undo stress on women labeled as infertile. Therefore, infertile Japanese women should be supported by psychiatric intervention.

In view of Immunology, natural-killer (NK) cell activity of the infertile Japanese women was significantly higher than that of the control. Elevated NK-cell activity is observed temporarily during stressful events. Persistent low NK-cell activity is associated with depression or stressful events caused by natural disasters. To the contrary, persistent high NK-cell activity is uncommon, however, increased NK-cell activity is observed in patients with recurrent pregnancy loss or Vietnam combat veterans diagnosed with long-term post-traumatic stress disorder (PTSD). A long-term chronic stress may underpin the basis for persistently high NK-cell activities. In consideration with high NK-cell activity for pregnancy, an embryo might be rejected from the uterus, because of its killing activity.

Therefore, a randomized study was performed to clarify the effects of psychiatric group intervention on the emotions, NK-cell activity and pregnancy rate in infertile Japanese women. Thirty-seven women completed a 5-session intervention program and were compared with 37 controls. Psychological discomfort and NK-cell activity significantly decreased after the intervention, whereas no significant changes were observed in controls. The pregnancy rate in the intervention group was significantly higher than that of controls. Psychological group intervention was effective in infertile Japanese women.

Finally, an interesting case was observed to achieve pregnant in a 50-year old Japanese woman with psychological relief. After failure of conception with 6 IVF attempts, the couple decided to discontinue further IVF treatment at age 48 years. One and one-half years later, she became pregnant naturally, resulting in getting healthy baby. During the time spanning her treatment for infertility, anxiety, depression, irritability, fatigue and grief were revealed to coexist with her high hopes of having a child. After termination of infertility treatments these adverse psychological findings were markedly lessened and her vigor was restored. Stopping infertility treatment might be a viable alternative for achieving pregnancy in similarly psychologically-challenged infertile women.

We believe that reproductive psychology will be one of the main topics in the field of fertility and sterility in the 21st century.

Keywords: anxiety, counselling, depression, infertility, NK cell activity

Particular Interests about Psychological Aspects in Infertile Japanese Women

In Japan, historically, women have been frequently asked such personal questions as 'Are you married? Do you have a child? How old are you?' without hesitation, because these are kinds of greeting. Old people sometimes blame women without children, because they think women should have heir and/or heiress with their family name, and because they still believe that infertility depends on only female cause. Moreover, media sometimes overreacts the new technologies of fertilization (e.g. in vitro fertilization and embryo transfer, intracytoplasmic sperm injection, or preimplantation genetic diagnosis), which might let patients being ashamed of infertility. We can easily assume that infertile Japanese women have high stress level. Little attention, however, has been paid to the psychological issue for the couples involved in Japan. For instance, the Japan Society of Obstetrics and Gynecology has never had psychological sessions for infertility at the annual meeting over a decade. Few studies of psychological aspects in infertile women have been published in Japan, whereas hundreds of articles were published in the western world [1]. In the western world, psychological care for infertile patients seems inevitable, but we have few infertility clinics thinking about psychological care, few psychiatrists or psychologists for infertility and lack of their education systems in Japan.

Impact of Psychological Distress in Infertile Japanese Women

The psychological problems most commonly investigated are anxiety and depression; anxiety because of the stressful nature of the treatment procedures, fear that treatment will fail [2]; and depression because of the patients' inability to conceive [3]. Most studies were performed in the western world, but contemporary studies showed similar psychological findings for infertile women from other countries such as Iran [4], Korea [5], and Taiwan [6].

How is this distress level in infertile Japanese women? A cross-sectional questionnaire study was performed to assess the psychological states of 101 infertile women (32.9±4.3 y/o; mean±SD, range 24-43), who had infertility history with more than 1 year (58.9±40.0 months, range 1-18 year), compared to 81 healthy pregnant women (30.5±4.2 y/o, range 23-41) [7]. In this study, the infertile women with history of any live birth, history of any psychiatric disorders and with other physical diseases concomitantly were excluded; the pregnant women whose current pregnancy have any concern (e.g. growth restriction, macrosomia, placenta previa, threatened abortion, or preterm labor) as well as women with a history of any psychiatric disorder, intra uterine fetal death of 2nd or 3rd trimester of previous pregnancy, and hereditary disease, were completely excluded. In order to detect emotional states, the Hospital Anxiety and Depression Scale (HADS [8]) and the Profile of Mood States (POMS [9]) were administered. The subjects filled in those questionnaires during waiting at the outpatient clinic and returned. The Japanese version of HADS was translated and validated by Kitamura [10], which can produce anxiety and depression. The total HADS scores distinguish between with or without emotional disorders with the cutoff of 12/13 (92% sensitivity and 90% specificity [11]). In terms of the POMS, that can produce the scores of depression/dejection, aggression/hostility, lack of vigor, fatigue, tension anxiety, confusion, and total mood disturbances. The Japanese version of the POMS was translated and standardized by Yokoyama [12].

Table 1. The HADS and the POMS scores between infertile and pregnant women

Scores	Infertile	Pregnant	P value[*]
HADS-Depression	4.6±2.9	3.5±2.1	0.003
HADS-Anxiety	6.9±3.1	5.3±3.0	0.0007
HADS (total)	11.6±5.2	8.8±4.2	0.0002
Depression/Dejection	10.9±8.7	5.0±4.9	<0.0001
Aggression/Hostility	9.4±7.3	7.2±5.5	0.02
Lack of Vigor	29.4±5.8	26.2±5.0	0.0001
Fatigue	8.3±5.9	8.2±5.0	NS
Tension Anxiety	10.4±6.1	7.6±5.4	0.001
Confusion	7.9±4.2	6.3±3.0	0.005
Total Mood Disturbances	76.3±28.8	60.4±19.3	<0.0001

Data are shown as mean values ± SD.
[*]Unpaired Student-t test was used between groups.
NS = not significant.

(Matsubayashi H, Hosaka T, Izumi S, Suzuki T, Makino T: Emotional distress of infertile women in Japan. Hum Reprod 2001; 16(5):966-969. ©European Society of Human Reproduction and Embryology. Reproduced by permission of Oxford University Press / Human Reproduction.)

Table 2. Positive percentage of total HADS scores in infertile and pregnant women

Cutoff	12/13	P value[*]
Infertile	38.6% (39/101)	0.0008
Pregnant	16.0% (13/81)	-

[*]χ2 test compared to pregnant women.

(Matsubayashi H, Hosaka T, Izumi S, Suzuki T, Makino T: Emotional distress of infertile women in Japan. Hum Reprod 2001; 16(5):966-969. ©European Society of Human Reproduction and Embryology. Reproduced by permission of Oxford University Press / Human Reproduction.)

In this population of Japanese women, all parameters of both the HADS and the POMS except for fatigue score from infertile women were significantly greater than those of healthy pregnant women (Table 1). In other word, these results suggested that infertile women were more likely have higher level of depression, dejection, anxiety, aggression, hostility, lack of vigor, tension anxiety, and confusion. Moreover, infertile women with positive HADS indicating emotional disorders (39/101, 38.6%) were significantly (p = 0.0008, χ2test) more than those of pregnant women (13/81, 16.0%) when the cutoff was set at 12/13 of total HADS scores (Table 2). The HADS scores were not affected by their age, duration of infertility, experience of conception, routine tests, and work states.

Our results are consistent with the previous studies in the western world. We, however, cannot compare directly this distress level of infertile Japanese women with those of other countries. It is clear that the infertile women have high emotional distress levels, especially with regard to anxiety and depression, suggesting that they would better be psychologically supported.

NATURAL-KILLER CELL ACTIVITY OF INFERTILE JAPANESE WOMEN

We focused on the Natural killer (NK) cell activity in order to connect psychiatry/psychology with immunology, because some reports showed that decreased NK activity has been associated with depression [13-15], and because NK cells are implicated in the immune responses associated with reproduction. For example, NK activity is abnormally low in patients with endometriosis and unusually high in women with unexplained recurrent miscarriages [16]. Might increased NK cell activity be involved in rejection of the embryo by interfering with successful invasion of trophoblast in the uterine endometrium? Since the mechanisms responsible for early pregnancy loss and infertility might overlap, we asked if infertile women had raised NK activity.

We tested 94 infertile women (34.6 years, range 28-44), who had a history of more than one year of infertility (5.9 years, range 2-18), and who despite treatment were unable to conceive for six or more months (2.4 years, range 0.5-10) [17]. None had a previous live birth or recurrent pregnancy loss. Controls were 94 age-matched, non-pregnant healthy female volunteers with no history of miscarriages or other diseases. Controls were sexually active and denied use of oral contraceptives, intra-uterine devices, or having undergone sterilization. All women were asked to complete two questionnaires, the HADS and the POMS. NK activity was measured by using a chromium-51 release cytotoxicity assay, with K562 human myeloid leukemia cells as targets (E/T=20/1). The percent cytotoxicity was calculated as ([test cpm - spontaneous cpm]/ [maximum cpm- spontaneous cpm]) x 100, where cpm = counts per minute. The percent cytotoxicity was interpreted to reflect NK activity. The NK activity of the infertile group (mean ± SD; 40.2% ± 14.7) was significantly higher than the control group (31.5% ± 11.9, P<0.0001) (Figure 1). The increased NK activity was not associated with age, infertile duration, depression scores, treated hyperprolactinemia, or treated endometriosis.

Elevated NK-cell activity is observed temporarily during stressful events [18-20]. Persistent low NK-cell activity is associated with depression [13-15] or stressful events caused by natural disasters [21,22]. To the contrary, persistent high NK-cell activity is uncommon, however, increased NK-cell activity is observed in patients with recurrent pregnancy loss or Vietnam combat veterans diagnosed with long-term post-traumatic stress disorder (PTSD [23]). A long-term chronic stress may underpin the basis for persistently high NK-cell activities. In consideration with high NK-cell activity for pregnancy, an embryo might be rejected from the uterus, because of its killing activity.

The response to stress is variable in different types of persons. Stress increases NK activity in the highly emotionally stable, low anxiety group, whereas stress decreases NK activity in the emotionally less stable, high anxiety group [18]. Interestingly, in murine models there is a genetic determinant in response to stress that causes infertility in A/J strain mice, and abortions in C3H strain mice [24]. These findings suggest that infertile patients with high NK activity might have some specific characteristics that have escaped evaluation to date. Moreover, the animal models would lend support to our findings that the reported increases in stress and NK activity associated with miscarriages in certain patients may provoke infertility in others.

INFERTILITY CAUSED BY DEPRESSION AND/OR ANXIETY

Infertility ranks as the fourth worst life event in severity, more so than death of ones' parents or unfaithfulness of ones' partners [25]. Anxiety comes from the stressful nature of the treatment procedures [26-28] and from fear that treatment will fail [2], whereas depression comes from the patients' inability to conceive [3]. Most studies have suggested that infertility and/or infertility treatment is an underlying source of psychological distress, but other recent studies have concluded that stress may be a causal factor leading to infertility [29-33]. Preexisting anxiety and/or depression are negatively associated with successful conception [7,34,35]. Counseling also has been reported to be effective in reducing anxiety and depression [36-38] and can result in successful conception [38-40]. Therefore, relief from stress could reduce the HADS score in infertile Japanese women.

The mechanism leading infertility with increased depression and anxiety may be explained by a link between hormonal changes and the psychological states; because there are some evidences showing the anxiety-induced hyperprolactinemia and failure to conceive [41,42], or because there are other evidences showing that the changes in prolactin, cortisol and testosterone provoked by a motional stressor vary with anxiety and depression [43,44]. It has been reported that anxiety causes uterine contraction at the time of embryo transfer, leading not to conceive [45].

EFFECT OF PSYCHIATRIC GROUP INTERVENTION ON INFERTILE JAPANESE WOMEN

Is the counseling also effective in infertile Japanese women? We investigated, for the first time in Japan, the effects of psychiatric group intervention on the emotions, natural-killer (NK) cell activity and pregnancy rate in infertile Japanese women by a randomized study [46]. We recruited 100 infertile Japanese women who had a history of more than one year of infertility and who, despite treatment, had been unable to conceive for six or more months. Patients who had any previous live births or recurrent pregnancy loss were excluded. With written consent, they were randomly assigned to the intervention or the control group. The intervention group consisted of 9 to 10 patients, and once it was formed, the program proceeded without changing the members. The intervention program consists of 5 weekly 90-minute sessions led by two professionals such as a psychiatrist and a nurse. Each session includes psycho-education, problem-solving, psychological support, relaxation training, and guided imagery. Each theme of psycho-education was: 1) general concepts of stress; 2) stress coping; 3) stress in infertile women; 4) immune function in infertile women; and 5) relationship between stress and immune function. In terms of problem-solving and psychological support, participants were facilitated to freely talk and discuss on difficulties in daily life, share information and mutually support. Participants were conducted to perform progressive muscle training and autogenic training, followed by guided imagery in which they were instructed to image insemination, implantation, growth of a fetus, and so on. These procedures were written as a manual form, therefore this can be called as a structured group intervention. The patients were administered the POMS and the HADS, and plasma samples for NK-cell activity were drawn before the 1st session and after the 5th session. NK-cell activity was also measured as above. This study was approved by the Institutional Review Board of the Tokai University School of Medicine.

Among 100 recruited infertile Japanese women, 2 patients became pregnant before the study, and 18 refused to participate. Therefore, 80 patients were assigned to each group. In the intervention group, 37 women completed the 5 sessions, 3 patients dropped out. In the control group, data at 5 weeks were not obtained from 3 patients. As a result, both group consisted of 37 infertile women. Between the groups, there were no significant differences in age (34.9 vs. 34.7 years old), duration of infertility (6.0 vs. 5.9 years), body weight (48.5 vs. 49.8 kg), initial scores of the HADS or the POMS, and NK-cell activity (unpaired Student's t-test). After the 5th session, the scores of depression, lack-of-vigor, aggression-hostility, fatigue and total mood disturbances from the POMS, and the anxiety and the total scores from the HADS decreased significantly compared with those before the 1st session (Table 3, paired Student's t-test). Interestingly, NK-cell activity was also decreased after the 5th session (Table 3, $P<0.0001$: paired Student's t-test). There, however, were no significant differences in the control group (data not shown). All women from each group have been followed up for 1 year after the intervention was completed. The pregnancy rate in the intervention group (14/37, 37.8%) was significantly higher than that of the control group (5/37, 13.5%, Table 4, χ^2 test, p=0.016).

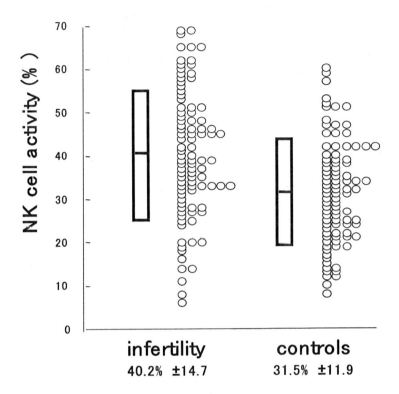

Figure 1. NK cell activity between infertile and control groups.
Box indicates mean ± SD of NK cell activity.
P<0.0001 (by two-tailed unpaired t-test).
(Matsubayashi H, Hosaka T, Sugiyama Y, Suzuki T, Arai T, Kondo A, Sugi T, Izumi
S-I, Makino T. Increased naturak-killer-cell activity is associated with infertile women.
Am J Reprod Immunol 2001; 46:318-322. ©Munksgaard, 2001. Reproduced by
permission of Blackwell Publishing Ltd. / American Journal of Reproductive
Immunology.)

According to the results in psychological inventories, our structured group
intervention was effective for alleviating the psychological discomfort (e.g.,
anxiety, depression) of our infertile Japanese women. Interestingly, such
psychological discomfort and high NK-cell activity were linked in our infertile
Japanese women. Since NK cells are rich in decidual tissue and high NK-cell
activity is associated with embryonal rejection, increased NK-cell activity
might have an unfavorable effect on maintaining pregnancy. In this context,
reducing high-NK-cell activity in infertile women might increase pregnancy
rate.

Table 3. Profile of Mood States (POMS), Hospital Anxiety and Depression Scale (HADS), and Natural-Killer (NK)-cell activity before and after psychological group intervention in the intervention group

	Pre-intervention	Post-intervention	P value*
POMS			
Depression	17.3±9.6	12.2±11.6	0.0036
Lack-of-Vigor	29.3±5.6	25.5±6.8	0.0002
Aggression-Hostility	13.8±8.8	10.5±9.2	0.0254
Fatigue	11.6±6.0	9.3±6.5	0.0234
Tension-Anxiety	12.9±6.9	11.2±7.3	0.0829
Confusion	9.5±4.3	8.4±4.2	0.0930
Total Mood Disturbances	94.1±30.6	77.0±35.4	0.0008
HADS			
Anxiety	7.2±3.1	5.9±3.0	0.0009
Depression	4.8±2.9	3.9±2.9	0.0527
Total	12.0±5.6	9.8±5.4	0.0019
NK-cell activity	47.7±16.7	34.1±15.7	<0.0001

*Paired Student's t-test.

(Hosaka T, Matsubayashi H, Sugiyama Y, Izumi S, Makino T: Effect of psychiatric group intervention on natural-killer-cell activity and pregnancy rate. Gen Hosp Psychiatry 2002; 24(5):353-356. ©2002 Elsevier Science Inc. Reproduced by permission of Elsevier / General Hospital Psychiatry.)

AN INTERESTING CASE IN WHICH PSYCHOLOGICAL RELIEF SEEMS TO ACHIEVE PREGNANT

Finally, an interesting case was observed to achieve pregnant in a 50-year old Japanese woman with psychological relief [47].

A healthy, nulligravid woman married at age 45 experienced two early pregnancy losses at ages 46 and 47. The first loss was at eight weeks (positive fetal heart tones) and the second loss was at seven weeks (blighted ovum) of gestation. After her second miscarriage, at 47 years 3 months of age, she presented to our infertility clinic. She and her husband hoped to have their child without delay. Her husband's semen analyses showed slightly asthenozospermia (40-45%) but total motile sperm was almost normal (20-28x10^6). She opted to circumvent our routine work-up for infertility except for hormonal tests because she had had two documented pregnancies, and, in view of her age, she did not want to undergo the usual tests for recurrent pregnancy loss. Her menstrual cycle historically had been 30 days, but it was irregular during the past 2 years (20-60 days cycle). Ultrasound examination revealed her uterus and both ovaries to be unremarkable. Her basal follicle-stimulating hormone (FSH) level was normal (3.4 IU/L), and she did not have hyperprolactinemia or a luteal phase defect. She didn't have psychiatric disorders.

During first 4 months, she was advised to have coitus at the day of ovulation monitored by ultrasound, but not pregnant. In succeeding 3 months, intrauterine insemination with her husband's sperm was performed in view of asthenozospermia, but failed to conceive. She and her husband did request IVF-ET. Their rationale for this choice was that IVF-ET procedure had the highest pregnancy success rate among infertility treatments, and that the residual oocytes might not be much in her age. A clomiphene-citrate-challenge test was performed that showed a good response for FSH (3.4 IU/L to 24.7 IU/L). Since there was no significant difference between clomiphene citrate plus gonadotropins and gonadotropin-releasing hormone (GnRH) agonist combined with gonadotropins for patients over 40 in our institute, the former was selected for ovarian stimulation. The first attempt for IVF resulted in no oocyte retrieval from either ovary. In the second and third oocyte retrieval attempts, embryo transfers with Veeck-graded 3 and 2 embryos respectively (only one embryo per each cycle) were unsuccessful. After these three consecutive attempts, she became anovulatory. Two cycles of hormone replacement therapy were instituted, but the fourth and fifth oocyte recovery attempts were abandoned as no growing follicles were detected. Her basal FSH level was 41.6 IU/L at age 48 years, 6 months. Another two cycles of hormone replacement therapy were performed to obtain reduced FSH levels (8.7 IU/L). To maintain the lower levels of FSH for the sixth retrieval attempt, a long-GnRH agonist protocol combined with gonadotropins was performed, but only one degenerated oocyte was retrieved. In summary, no pregnancy was achieved after two embryo transfers were performed as a result of four oocyte retrieval attempts and six ovarian stimulation cycles.

After frank discussions about future expectations regarding additional infertility treatments, she and her husband concluded that they should cease further IVF treatment. Their decision was based upon the wife's poor response to ovarian stimulation, inferior-grade oocytes and prohibition of donor oocytes usage in Japan. At age 48 years, 10 months she and her husband stopped infertility clinic visits and she quit monitoring her basal body temperature.

128   Hidehiko Matsubayashi, Takashi Hosaka and Tsunehisa Makino

Table 4. Pregnancy rate in the intervention group and the control group

	Intervention group	Control group
Pregnancy rate	14/37 (37.8%)	5/37 (13.5%)
	P=0.016(χ^2 test)	

(Hosaka T, Matsubayashi H, Sugiyama Y, Izumi S, Makino T: Effect of psychiatric
group intervention on natural-killer-cell activity and pregnancy rate. Gen Hosp
Psychiatry 2002; 24(5):353-356. ©2002 Elsevier Science Inc. Reproduced by
permission of Elsevier / General Hospital Psychiatry.)

One and one half years later at age 50 years, 3 months, she appeared at our
clinic to say she might be pregnant. Her menstrual cycle was also irregular
(20-60 days cycle). At that time, her pregnancy was eight weeks gestation and
she complained of a slight emesis. She was afraid of a fetal anomaly because
she had taken several drugs for a common cold. We discussed the risk of fetal
anomalies resulting from the drugs and her additional risks due to her age.
After contemplating pregnancy termination, the couple chose to have the baby.
Between 10 and 14 weeks of gestation she was admitted to our hospital for a
threatened abortion and hyperemesis gravidarum. Her thyroid function was
normal. The couple declined amniocentesis because they had decided to have
this baby regardless of the outcome. After that, her pregnancy was uneventful.
She was delivered at 38 weeks gestation of a 2740g (6 lb.) infant with Apgar
scores of 9 and 10. The infant was healthy without any abnormalities.

While pregnant, she agreed to participate in our questionnaire with visual
analogue scales (VAS) designed to ascertain retrospective information about
her psychological well-being for the past three years. The aim of this
questionnaire is to see changing of feeling with this period, which is not
absolute but relative. Her responses revealed that her aspirations for having
children had continued unabated during this period (Figure 2). Her husband
remained supportive throughout this period. Feelings of pressure were scored
as consistently neutral. Tension scores were decreased temporally when her
infertility treatments were discontinued, but reappeared before she became
pregnant. Anxiety, depression, irritability, fatigue and grief were markedly
reduced after stopping her infertility treatments and her vigor was restored to
normal values.

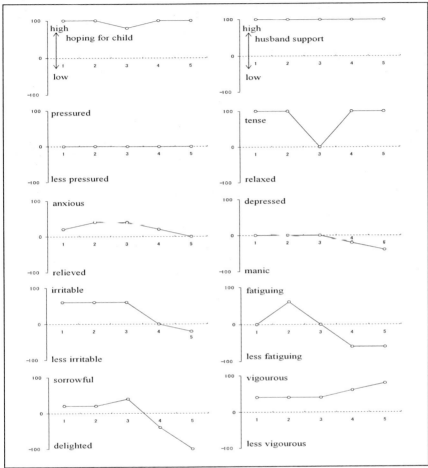

Figure 2. Assessment of patient feelings by using our original questionnaire with visual analog scale. We asked the patient to retrospectively describe her feelings before, during and after infertility treatments, two months prior to conception and surrounding conception. For example, 'If you set most delighted experience at +100 and most sorrowful experience at -100, express your feeling between -100 and 100 at each time'. 1; before visiting our infertility clinic, 2; during infertility treatments, 3; after quitting infertility treatments, 4; two months before conception, 5; surrounding conception. (Matsubayashi H, Iwasaki K, Suzuki T, Izumi S-I, Makino T. Spontaneous Conception in a 50-year Old Woman after Giving up In-Vitro-Fertilization (IVF) Treatments: Involvement of the Psychological Relief in Successful Pregnancy. Tokai J Exp Clin Med 2003; 28(1):9-15. © The Tokai Journal of Experimental and Clinical Medicine. Reproduced by permission of the Tokai Journal of Experimental and Clinical Medicine.)

Infertility or infertility treatment is a source of psychological distress, but this may be a causal factor for infertility at the same time. Most Japanese Gynecologist believe and advise that women over 40 years old who want to have their children should choose IVF-ET in earlier convenience. Once IVF-ET was performed, however, it is difficult to cease IVF-ET, because we don't have other option to give such older women. The psychological relief seems to be observed in our patient after stopping infertility treatment followed by successful conception. This case suggests that simple continuation of IVF treatment may not be appropriate to achieve pregnant for such older women and that quitting IVF treatment does not always mean giving up being pregnant, because psychological factor cannot be excluded. Since studies assessing emotional well-being, infertility and fecundity have yet to be published for women who don't come to infertility clinic, we hope that this case report will stimulate others to explore this potential.

CONCLUSION

Reproductive psychology is just the beginning in the reproductive field. Gynecologists should pay more attention to such field. We believe that reproductive psychology will be one of the main topics in the field of fertility and sterility in the 21st century.

ACKNOWLEDGMENTS

In order to review the psychological issue in Japan and to prepare this paper, copyright permission is granted from the following publishers:

Matsubayashi H, Hosaka T, Sugiyama Y, Suzuki T, Arai T, Kondo A, Sugi T, Izumi S-I, Makino T. Increased naturak-killer-cell activity is associated with infertile women. Am J Reprod Immunol 2001; 46:318-322. ©Munksgaard, 2001. Reproduced by permission of Blackwell Publishing Ltd. / American Journal of Reproductive Immunology.

Hosaka T, Matsubayashi H, Sugiyama Y, Izumi S, Makino T: Effect of psychiatric group intervention on natural-killer-cell activity and pregnancy rate. Gen Hosp Psychiatry 2002; 24(5):353-356. ©2002 Elsevier Science Inc. Reproduced by permission of Elsevier / General Hospital Psychiatry.

Matsubayashi H, Hosaka T, Izumi S, Suzuki T, Makino T: Emotional distress of infertile women in Japan. Hum Reprod 2001; 16(5):966-969.

REFERENCES

[1]   Greil AL. Infertility and psychological distress: a critical review of the literature. *Soc Sci Med* 45:1679-1704, 1997.

[2]   Cook R, Parsons J, Mason B, Golombok S. Emotional, marital and sexual functioning in patients embarking upon IVF and AID treatment for infertility. *J Reprod Infant Psychol* 7:87-93, 1989.

[3]   Golombok S. Psychological functioning in infertility patients. *Hum Reprod* 7:208-212, 1992.

[4]   Nasseri M. Cultural similarities in psychological reactions to infertility. *Psychol Rep* 86:375-378, 2000.

[5]   Kee BS, Jung BJ, Lee SH. A study on psychological strain in IVF patients. *J Assist Reprod Genet* 17:445-448, 2000.

[6]   Lee T-Y, Sun G-H, Chao S-C. The effect of an infertility diagnosis on the distress, marital and sexual satisfaction between husbands and wives in Taiwan. *Hum Reprod* 16:1762-1767, 2001.

[7]   Matsubayashi H, Hosaka T, Izumi S, Suzuki T, Makino T: Emotional distress of infertile women in Japan. *Hum Reprod* 16:966-969, 2001.

[8]   Zigmond AS and Snaith RP. The Hospital Anxiety and Depression Scale. *Acta Psychiatr Scand*, 67:361-370, 1983.

[9]   McNair DM, Lorr M and Droppleman LF. (eds) *Manual for the Profile of Mood States. Educational and Industrial Testing Service*, San Diego, 1971.

[10] Kitamura T. Hospital Anxiety and Depression Scale. *Seishinka Shindangaku (Diagnostic Psychiatry),* 4:371-372, 1993 (in Japanese).

[11] Hosaka T, Awazu H, Aoki T, et al. Screening for adjustment disorders and major depression in otolaryngology patients using the Hospital Anxiety and Depression Scale. *Intl J Psychiatr Clin Prac*, 3:43-48, 1999.

132   Hidehiko Matsubayashi, Takashi Hosaka and Tsunehisa Makino

[12] Yokoyama K and Araki S. Japanese edition of Profile of Mood States (POMS). *Kaneko Shobou*, 1994 (in Japanese).

[13] Herbert TB, Cohen S. Depression and immunity: a meta-analytic review. *Psychol Bull* 113:472-486, 1993.

[14] Marvin S, Miller AH, Trestman RL. Depression, the immune system, and health and illness. *Arch Gen Psychiatry* 48:171-177, 1991.

[15] Schleifer SJ, Keller SE, Bartlett JA, Eckholdt HM, Delaney BR. Immunity in young adults with major depressive disorder. *Am J Psychiatry* 153:477-482, 1996.

[16] Somigliana E, Vigano P, Vignali M. Endometriosis and unexplained recurrent spontaneous abortion: pathological states resulting from aberrant modulation of natural killer cell function? *Hum Reprod Update* 5:40-51, 1999.

[17] Matsubayashi H, Hosaka T, Sugiyama Y, Suzuki T, Arai T, Kondo A, Sugi T, Izumi S-I, Makino T. Increased naturak-killer-cell activity is associated with infertile women. *Am J Reprod Immunol*, 46:318-322, 2001.

[18] Borella P, Bargellini A, Rovesti S, Pinelli M, Vivoli R, Solfrini V, Vivoli G. Emotional stability, anxiety, and natural killer activity under examination stress. *Psychoneuroendocrinology* 24:613-627, 1999.

[19] Dopp JM, Miller GE, Myers HF, Fahey JL. Increased natural killer-cell mobilization and cytotoxicity during marital conflict. *Brain Behav Immun* 14:10-26, 2000.

[20] Delahanty DL, Wang T, Maravich C, Forlenza M, Baum A. Time-of-day effects on response of natural killer cells to acute stress in men and women. *Health Psychol* 19:39-45, 2000.

[21] Solomon GF, Segerstorm SC, Grohr P, Kemeny M, Fahey J. Shaking up immunity: Psychological and immunlogic changes after a natural disaster. *Psychosom Med* 59:114-127, 1997.

[22] Ironson G, Wynings C, Schneiderman N, Baum A, Rodriguez M, Greenwood D, Benight C, Antoni M, LaPerriere A, Huang HS, Klimas N, Fletcher MA. Posttraumatic Stress Symptoms, intrusive thoughts, loss, and immune function after Hurricane Andrew. *Psychosom Med* 59:128-141, 1997.

[23] Laudenslager ML, Aasal R, Adler L, Berger CL, Montgomery PT, Sandberg E, Wahlberg LJ, Wilkins RT, Zweig L, Reite ML. Elevated cytotoxicity in combat veterans with long-term post-traumatic stress disorder: preliminary observations. *Brain Behav Immun* 12:74-79, 1998.

[24] Clark DA, Banwatt D, Chaouat G. Stress-triggered abortion in mice prevented by alloimmunization. *Am J Reprod Immunol* 29:141-147, 1993.

[25] Oddens BJ, Tonkelaar I, Nieuwenhuyse H. Psychosocial experiences in women facing fertility problems. *Hum Reprod* 14:255-261, 1999.

[26] Eimers JM, Omtzigt AM, Vogelzang ET, van Ommen R, Habbema DF, te Velde ER. Physical complaints and emotional stress related to routine diagnostic procedures of the fertility investigation. *J Psychosom Obstet Gynecol* 18:31-35, 1997.

[27] Lukse MP and Vacc NA. Grief, depression, and coping in women undergoing infertility treatment. *Obstet Gynecol* 93:245-251, 1999.

[28] Yong P, Martin C, Thong J. A comparison of psychological functioning in women at different stages of in vitro fertilization treatment using the mean affect adjective check list. *J Assist Reprod Genet* 17:553-556, 2000.

[29] Gallinelli A, Roncaglia R, Matteo ML, Ciaccio I, Volpe A, Facchinetti F. Immunological changes and stress are associated with different implantation rates in patients undergoing in vitro fertilization-embryo transfer. *Fertil Steril* 76:85-91, 2001.

[30] Klonoff-Cohen H, Chu E, Natarajan L, Sieber W. A prospective study of stress among women undergoing in vitro fertilization or gamete intrafallopian transfer. *Fertil Steril* 76:675-687, 2001.

[31] Sanders KA and Bruce NW. A prospective study of psychosocial stress and fertility in women. *Hum Reprod* 12:2324-2329, 1997.

[32] Csemiczky G, Landgren BM, Collins A. The influence of stress and state anxiety on the outcome of IVF-treatment: Psychological and endocrinological assessment of Swedish women entering IVF-treatment. *Acta Obstet Gynecol Scand* 79:113-118, 2000.

[33] Sanders KA and Bruce NW. Psychosocial stress and treatment outcome following assisted reproductive technology. *Hum Reprod* 14:1652-1662, 1999.

[34] Smeenk JMJ, Verhaak CM, Eugster A, van Minnen A, Zielhuis GA, Braat DDM. The effect of anxiety and depression on the outcome of in-vitro fertilization. *Hum Reprod* 16:1420-1423, 2001.

[35] Demyttenaere K, Bonte L, Gheldof M, et al. Coping style and depression level influence outcome in in vitro fertilization. *Fertil Steril* 69:1026-1033, 1998.

[36] Domar AD, Zuttermeister PC, Seibel MM, Benson H. Psychological improvement in infertile women after behavioral treatment: a replication. *Fertil Steril* 58:144-147, 1992.

[37] Domar AD, Clapp D, Slawsby E, Kessel B, Orav J, Freizinger M. The impact of group psychological interventions on distress in infertile women. *Health Psychol* 19:568-575, 2000.

[38] Terzioglu F. Investigation into effectiveness of counseling on assisted reproductive techniques in Turkey. *J Psychosom Obstet Gynaecol* 22:133-141, 2001.

[39] Sarrel PM and DeCherney AH. Psychotherapeutic intervention for treatment of couples with secondary infertility. *Fertil Steril* 43:897-900, 1985.

[40] Domar AD, Clapp D, Slawsby EA, Dusek J, Kessel B, Freizinger M. Impact of group psychological interventions on pregnancy rates in infertile women. *Fertil Steril* 73:805-812, 2000.

[41] Edelmann RJ and Golombok S. Stress and reproductive failure. *J Reprod Infant Osychol* 7:79-86, 1989.

[42] Harrison RF, O'Moore RR, O'Moore AM. Stress and fertility: some modalities of investigation and treatment in couples with unexplained infertility in Dublin. *Int J Fertil* 31, 153-159, 1986.

[43] Merari D, Feldberg D, Elizur A, et al. Psychological and hormonal changes in the course of in vitro fertilization. *J Assist Repro Genet* 9, 161-169, 1992.

[44] Demyttenaere K, Nijs P, Evers-Kiebooms G, et al. The effect of specific emotional stressor on prolactine, cortisol and testosterone concentrations in women varies with their trait anxiety. *Fertil Steril* 52, 942-948, 1989.

[45] Fanchin R, Gellman S, Righini C, Ayoubi JM, Olivennes F, Frydman R. Uterine contraction frequency at the time of embryo transfer (ET) is correlated with anxiety levels [abstract no. P499]. In: *Program and abstracts of the 56th Annual Meeting of the American Society for Reproductive Medicine*. San Diego, CA: Fertil Steril 2000; 74: S252.

[46] Hosaka T, Matsubayashi H, Sugiyama Y, Izumi S, Makino T: Effect of psychiatric group intervention on natural-killer-cell activity and pregnancy rate. *Gen Hosp Psychiatry* 24:353-356, 2002.

[47] Matsubayashi H, Iwasaki K, Suzuki T, Izumi S-I, Makino T. Spontaneous Conception in a 50-year Old Woman after Giving up In-Vitro-Fertilization (IVF) Treatments: Involvement of the Psychological Relief in Successful Pregnancy. *Tokai J Exp Clin Med* 28:9-15,2003.

In: Psychological Distress   ISBN: 978-1-61942-646-7
Editors: H. Ohayashi and S. Yamada   © 2012 Nova Science Publishers, Inc.

Chapter 8

PSYCHOLOGICAL DISTRESS AND QUALITY OF LIFE AMONG PATIENTS WITH GYNECOLOGIC CANCER[*]

Mika Kobayashi[1,2], Tatsuya Ohno[3,4,†], Wataru Noguchi[1], Toshiko Matsushita[5] and Eisuke Matsushima[1]
[1]Department of Comprehensive Diagnosis and Therapeutics, Section of Liaison Psychiatry & Palliative Medicine, Graduate School of Tokyo Medical and Dental University, Tokyo, Japan
[2]Department of Social Psychiatry, National Institute of Mental Health, National Center of Neurology and Psychiatry, Tokyo, Japan
[3]Research Center for Charged Particle Therapy, National Institute of Radiological Sciences, Chiba, Japan
[4]Gunma University Heavy Ion Medical Center, Gunma, Japan. 3-39-22 Showa-machi, Maebashi, Gunma 371-8511, Japan
[5]Department of Health and Medical Care, Saitama Medical University, Saitama, Japan

---

[*] A version of this chapter also appears in *New Perspectives on Women and Depression*, edited by William Hansson and Erik Olsson, published by Nova Science Publishers, Inc. It was submitted for appropriate modifications in an effort to encourage wider dissemination of research.
[†] Tel: +81-27-220-8378.Fax: +81-27-220-8379. E-mail: tohno@gunma-u.ac.jp

ABSTRACT

Being diagnosed and treated for gynecologic cancer is an enormous physical and psychological challenge for the individual woman. During the course of treatment and even after, many patients deal with further life crises. In addition to the general stress caused by cancer, patients with gynecologic cancer can be vulnerable to distress associated with damage to self-image, altered sexual function, and loss of fertility. We conducted 3 studies on the theme of psychological distress among gynecologic cancer patients. Our results showed that patients experienced anger, fear, depression and anxiety, and we recommend early psychosocial intervention for reduction of stressors, enhancing coping skills to manage stressors that cannot be reduced or removed, and establishment of a mental state and support system to maximize adaptation.

INTRODUCTION

Gynecologic cancer accounts for 11.5% of all cancers in women [1]. Sites include the cervix, ovaries, endometrium, vulva, and vagina. For gynecologic cancer patients, the cancer and the treatment effects will usually affect issues involving femininity, self-image, sexual function, and fertility, as well as the general distress that accompanies any cancer treatment [2]. As such, many of the patients are confronted with psychological distress and their quality of life (QOL) is often disturbed during the course of treatment and many patients will eventually deal with further life crises even after the treatment is completed.

Gynecologic cancer is often treated with multiple treatment modalities [3]. The standard treatment for gynecological cancer has been changing with tremendous speed. A randomized study showed that radiotherapy for early (Stage Ib and IIa) cervical cancer was equally effective as radical surgery, with a 5-year overall survival of 83% [4][5]. Patients with advanced stages of cervical cancer can have external pelvic radiotherapy combined with brachytherapy to the cervix; currently, this therapy is usually combined with chemotherapy as well [6].

Previous studies indicated that different treatment modalities affected the lives of surviving women to varying degrees in terms of physical, sexual, and psychosocial functioning [6]. Therefore, to maintain or increase QOL in gynecologic cancer patients, careful consideration of all domains that can negatively affect QOL is required. This includes surgery, the side effects of chemotherapy and radiotherapy, and disease-associated factors. We have conducted three studies [7][8][9] on the theme of psychological distress and quality of life among gynecologic cancer patients with different treatment modalities.

1. EMOTIONAL STATE AND COPING STYLE AMONG GYNECOLOGIC CANCER PATIENTS UNDERGOING SURGERY [7]

Introduction

In this study of gynecologic patients, the emotional state in the perioperative period and the relationship between emotional state and other factors including coping style among gynecologic patients were investigated. Here, we report a portion of the total study, which are the perioperative changes in emotional states among gynecologic patients undergoing surgery irrespective of the presence or absence of cancer.

Methods

Sample

This was a prospective study that longitudinally followed 90 patients who were admitted to the Department of Obstetrics and Gynecology at Tokyo Medical and Dental University Hospital. During the recruitment phase (June 2002-March 2004), 98 patients met the inclusion criteria. Eight patients were excluded and 90 patients were eligible. The reasons for exclusion were as follows: two did not consent to participate, four subsequently withdrew consent or dropped out due to deterioration in physical condition and two died before discharge.

Demographic and medical variables are summarized in Table 1. Of 90 patients, 32 were diagnosed with benign disease (mean age, 41.0 ± 11.3 years) and 58 with malignancy (mean age, 50.2 ± 13.0 years). In the benign group, 16 had ovarian tumors, 10 had tubo-ovarian abscesses, and 6 had other tumors including cervical adenoma. In the malignant group, 28 had cervical cancer, 12 had uterine body cancer, and 18 had ovarian cancer. Patients at disease Stage 0, I, or II were classified as the early stage group (n=47), and those at Stages III or IV were classified as the advanced stage group (n=11). The two groups showed no significant differences in demographic and medical variables such as length of education, habituation status, employment status, or types of surgical treatments. By contrast, significant differences were observed in age, duration of hospitalization, and location of tumor.

Table 1. Patient characteristics: demographic variables (n=58).
Adapted from Matsushita et al. [7]

	Benign group (n=32)		Malignant group (n=58)		
	Mean/ Number	SD/%	Mean/Number	SD/%	P
Age (years)	41.0	11.3	50.2	13.0	0.0011
Length of education (years)	14.0	1.8	13.0	2.3	0.05666
Duration of hospitalization (days)	14.0	5.3	28.2	25.4	0.0025
Habituation status					0.8032
Single	6	18.8	12	20.7	
Spouse only	7	21.9	17	29.3	
Others	19	59.4	29	50.0	
Employment status					>0.999
Employed	13	40.6	24	41.4	
Unemployed	19	59.4	34	58.6	
Location of tumor					<0.0001
Uterine cervix	2	6.3	28	48.3	
Uterine body	1	3.1	12	20.7	
Ovary	29	90.6	18	31.0	
Progress					NA
Early	NA	NA	47	81.0	
Advanced	NA	NA	11	19.0	
Surgical Treatment					0.2812
Laparotomy	17	53.1	38	65.5	
Conization/ others	15	46.9	20	34.5	
Chemotherapy (+) / (-)	0/32	0/100	15/43	25.9/74.1	NA

Measure

A self-administered questionnaire, Japanese version of Profile of Mood States (POMS) was used for the study. The POMS [10][11][12] was used to measure six emotional states: tension-anxiety, depression, anger-hostility, vigor, fatigue, and confusion. A higher score (in the case of vigor, a lower score) indicated a more severe emotional state. These subscales were standardized according to the consecutive studies of Yokoyama and Araki, and the standardized scores were converted from raw scores in the study. The participants were asked to complete the questionnaire at Time 1 (T1), Time 2 (T2), and Time 3 (T3).

Results

Emotional states over the three test administration days

The POMS scores for all participants were within normal range at all times (Table 2).

Table 2. POMS subscale scores in the three groups.
Adapted from Matsushita et al. [7]

Subscales	Before surgery	Before discharge	3 months after discharge	F value	P value
Tension-anxiety	47.7±10.6	42.0±9.2	43.9±10.3	F=9.356	P=0.0001
Depression	46.3±9.0	44.0±6.6	47.8±10.8	F=6.819	P=0.0015
Anger-hostility	42.3±5.7	40.2±4.3	44.4±8.5	F=15.101	P<0.0001
Vigor	48.5±9.6	51.4±11.1	51.0±11.2	No Significant Difference	
Fatigue	43.3±9.1	43.0±9.6	44.7±9.7	No Significant Difference	
Confusion	44.4±10.5	42.1±8.8	45.3±11.5	F=3.956	P=0.0211

There were significant differences in the scores of tension-anxiety, depression, anger-hostility, and confusion across the three examination periods (tension-anxiety: F=9.356, P=0.0001; depression: F=6.819, P=0.0015; anger-hostility: F=15.101, P<0.0001; confusion: F=3.956, P=0.0211). There were no significant differences in the scores of vigor and fatigue across the study period. Also, the tension-anxiety score was the highest before surgery, and the depression, anger-hostility, and confusion scores were the highest after discharge. Furthermore, there were no significant differences in the POMS subscales between the three disease groups with the exception of anger-hostility. The anger-hostility score was the lowest in the advanced-stage group and the highest in the benign group (F=4.016, P=0.0220).

Discussion

Changes in Emotional State over the Study Period

Regarding changes in emotional state, the results showed that the patterns of depression and anger were different compared to anxiety. While anxiety was the highest before surgery, depression and anger were maximal at three months after discharge. High anxiety before surgery might be due to general concerns regarding the surgery itself. In contrast, high levels of depression and anger after discharge might be attributed to psychological distress associated with damage to self-image, altered sexual function, and loss of fertility [2, 13-21]. Such distress appears to be overt after discharge when the patient's physical condition has improved.

In a previous study by Matsushita [22], the psychological states of gastrointestinal patients undergoing surgery were examined. The results showed that depression scores increased from preoperative to postoperative, and depression continued six months after discharge while anxiety scores did not change across the study period. Matsushita's study supports the results of the present study with regard to the following two points: (i) depression changed significantly over the study period; and (ii) the pattern of anxiety was different from that of depression. These findings support the timely initiation of treatment or care for gynecologic patients. Medical staff should offer preoperative orientation and explanation about surgery to patients with gynecologic disease with special attention to their anxiety. Furthermore, follow-up psychological examinations should be conducted by psychiatrists or psychologists to evaluate patients' emotional states such as depression, anger, and confusion. A routine psychological screening test conducted at follow up might also be useful.

Incidence of Psychiatric Disease and the Level of Emotional State over the Study Period

The POMS average scores for all subjects were within the standard range for each subscale on three examination periods. Furthermore, only three of 90 subjects had psychological symptoms warranting psychiatric diagnosis. Therefore, the morbidity rate was relatively low at 3.3% when compared with findings from previous studies that investigated psychiatric morbidity rates among cancer patients.

Bodurka-Bevers et al. [23] investigated depression and anxiety among patients with ovarian cancer (26% had early stage cancer, 74% had advanced-stage cancer, and 49% were undergoing active treatment), and they reported that 21% of subjects had scores which exceeded the threshold for depression, and 29% of subjects had anxiety scores which exceeded 75% of the average. In the present study, the POMS average scores were all within the normal range. This could be explained by differences in the measurements tools. Also, the inclusion of subjects with benign tumors and patients with early stage disease outnumbered those with advanced-stage disease.

There were no differences in most POMS subscale scores between the benign, early stage, and advanced-stage groups. In the present study, the physical condition of the advanced-stage patients was not severe. Lutgendorf et al. [24] examined QOL and mood in women with gynecologic cancer at the initial clinic visit and after one year by using FACT (Functional Assessment of Cancer Therapy; measuring QOL) and POMS. Those results indicated that QOL and mood improved among the early stage and regionally advanced oncology patients and that there were no significant differences in mood between the two patient groups over time. Those findings support the present study. Irrespective of whether the patients have cancer or whether their cancer is at an early or at an advanced stage, the distress common to all gynecologic patients undergoing surgery might be associated with concerns other than surgery, cancer, or the disease itself.

Also, the anger-hostility score was higher in the benign group than in the advanced-stage group. Similar results in previous studies of gynecologic patients were not obtained. Gynecologic patients with benign disease have no fear of cancer; therefore they are not severely anxious. Feelings such as anger and hostility might be exhibited to a greater extent by these patients than by cancer patients. In fact, through clinical experience in gynecologic units we confirmed that strong negative emotions such as fear and anxiety often prevail over anger and hostility.

Conclusion

The study clarified perioperative changes in the emotional state among gynecologic patients undergoing surgery and the relationship between these and related factors. The majority of psychological variables changed over the perioperative period; therefore timely intervention with consideration of individual treatment conditions and situations is important.

2. PSYCHOLOGICAL DISTRESS AND QUALITY OF LIFE IN CERVICAL CANCER SURVIVORS AFTER RADIOTHERAPY: DO TREATMENT MODALITIES, DISEASE STAGE, AND SELF-ESTEEM INFLUENCE OUTCOMES? [8]

Introduction

Cervical cancer is the second most common cancer among women worldwide [25][26]. Survival rates of cervical cancer patients have been increasing because of earlier detection and more effective treatment programs [26], so that QOL among cervical cancer survivors has gained increasing attention.

Radiotherapy plays an important role in the treatment of cervical cancer patients. Previous studies indicated that different treatment modalities affected the lives of survivors to varying degrees in terms of physical, sexual, and psychosocial functioning [26]. Maintaining QOL for gynecologic cancer survivors after radiotherapy requires careful consideration of all domains that impact the patient. In terms of physical and psychosocial concerns among cervical cancer survivors, it has been difficult to draw definite conclusions, and many previous studies lacked information about the patients' disease stages and treatment modalities [26].

In addition to treatment modalities and disease stages, self-esteem can promote or detract from a patient's well being [27]. In the mid 1960s, Maurice Rosenberg defined self-esteem as a favorable or unfavorable attitude toward the self. This became the most frequently used definition for research [28]. A patient's self-esteem may influence his/her psychological distress; however, few studies have examined self-esteem in cancer survivors. This study aimed to evaluate psychological distress in cervical cancer survivors. We examined whether differences in treatment modalities, disease stages, and self-esteem influence psychological distress.

Methods

Research Center Hospital for Charged Particle Therapy at National Institute of Radiological Sciences research review board approved the study and granted formal access to the patients. Before participation, all participants were informed of the nature, risks, and benefits of study participation and written informed consent was obtained.

Subjects

Cervical cancer survivors were eligible for study participation if (1) they were older than 20 years; (2) they were aware of their cancer diagnosis; (3) they had a diagnosis of cervical cancer and had completed their cancer treatment at least six months before study participation; (4) their condition did not prevent completion of the questionnaire or participation in the study; (5) they had no severe mental disorder or dementia; and (6) they were able to provide informed consent.

All study subjects were requested to complete the questionnaires when they visited the hospital for their outpatient follow-up visits. Medical information and demographic data were taken from medical records and patient reports.

Hospital Anxiety and Depression Scale (HADS)

The HADS is a self-rated questionnaire with 14 items that measured psychological distress: anxiety (HADS-A) and depression (HADS-D) [29]. The Japanese version of HADS was back translated by Kitamura (1993) [30], and the reliability and the validity of the Japanese version of HADS was confirmed by Kugaya et al. (1998)[31]. Each item was based on a 4-point response scale (0 to 3) so the possible scores ranged from 0 to 21 for anxiety and 0 to 21 for depression [32]; the higher the score, the higher the level of symptoms. A total score on the HADS-D and HADS-A of 8 was defined as suspected depression and total a score of 11 or higher was considered indicative of depression [33][34].

Rosenberg Self-Esteem Scale (RSE)

Self-esteem was measured with the Japanese version of the Rosenberg Self-Esteem scale, a widely used, reliable, and valid measure [35]. The RSE measured the overall sense of being capable and feeling worthwhile and competent. The questionnaire consisted of 10 items, measured on a 5-point scale (1 to 5). The maximum score of 50 reflected the best possible self-esteem while the minimal score of 10 reflected the least possible self-esteem.

Statistical Analyses

We compiled descriptive statistics on psychological distress, self-esteem, and clinical and demographic measures.

In addition, differences in psychological distress among treatment modalities were analyzed using one-way analysis of variance (ANOVA) with post hoc comparisons (Scheffe F test). Differences in psychological distress depending on disease stages and self-esteem were analyzed using the Mann-Whitney U test. All p values were two-sided, and the significance level was set at $p<0.05$.

To examine the differences of psychological distress depending on disease stages, Stages I and II were categorized into an early stage group, and Stages III, IV and recurrence were categorized into an advanced stage group.

To examine the relationships of self-esteem scores and the scores of psychological distress, participants were divided into a higher self-esteem group (n=33; scores of RSE were higher than the median) and a low self-esteem group (n=31; scores of RSE were lower than the median). The median score of self-esteem was 35.0. The median score was selected for cutoff because there was no cutoff for the original Japanese version of the RSE for the cancer population. The scores were distributed binomially at the border of the median.

Results

During the recruitment phase (March 2005- September 2005), 72 patients met the inclusion criteria. Of these, 12 were excluded because of incomplete data and 60 were eligible.

Demographic and Medical Variables

Demographic and medical variables are summarized in Table 3.

The mean age was 61.4 years (range, 32–79 years, SD = 11.8). Mean length of education was 11.7 years, and 38 of 60 participants (63.3%) were married. Twenty-three patients (38.3%) had Stage III disease and 7 (11.7%) patients had Stage IV disease. Thirty-three patients (55.0%) received radiotherapy, 18 patients (30.0%) received chemoradiotherapy, and 9 patients (15.0%) received postoperative radiotherapy. Mean follow-up time of the patients was 33.0 months (range, 6.3 to 129.2 months) after initiation of treatment.

Differences of Psychological Distress among Treatment Modalities, Disease Stages, and Self-esteem

Psychological distress for each treatment modality is shown in Table 4.

There were no significant differences of scores for anxiety and depression among the three treatment modalities (HADS-A: $F=0.258$, $df=2$, $p=0.774$; HADS-D: $F=0.034$, $df=2$, $p=0.967$). Similarly, there were no significant differences in scores for anxiety and depression (Table 3) between the early stage group and the advanced stage group (HADS-A: $U=314.5$, $p=0.144$; HADS-D: $U=394.5$, $p=0.866$).

Discussion

The results of the present study indicate that differences in levels of psychological distress among cervical cancer survivors were not significant for treatment modalities and disease stages. However, scores for anxiety and depression were significantly different depending on the survivors' self-esteem.

Figure 1 shows that the scores of anxiety and depression in the high self-esteem group were significantly lower than those of the low self-esteem group (HADS-A: U=242.0, p=0.008; HADS-D: U=245.0, p=0.010).

Table 3. Patient characteristics (N=60) Adapted from Kobayashi et al. [8]

	No. (%)	Mean	SD
Age, yrs		61.4	11.8
Marital status			
Married	38 (63.3)		
Single	12 (20.0)		
Widowed	10 (16.7)		
Education, yrs		11.7	2.0
Occupation			
Employed full-time	15 (25.0)		
Employed part-time	8 (13.3)		
Unemployed	36 (60.0)		
Other	1 (1.7)		
Disease Stage			
0	1		
I	14		
II	14		
III	23		
IV	7		
Recurrence	1		
Treatment Modalities			
Radiation			
0	1		
I	8		
II	9		
III	14		
IV	0		
Recurrence	1		
Chemo + Radiation			
0	0		
I	3		
II	1		
III	9		
IV	5		
Recurrence	0		
Surgery+Radiation			
0	0		
I	3		
II	4		
III	0		
IV	1		
Recurrence	1		

Table 4. HADS Scores. Adapted from Kobayashi et al. [8]

Psychological Distress (HADS)		
	Anxiety	Depression
Treatment		
Radiation	5.0	4.5
Chemo + Radiation	4.6	4.7
Radiation+Surgery	3.8	4.0
Stage		
Early	4.0	4.2
Advanced	5.2	4.6
Self-esteem		
High	3.8 *	3.5 *
Low	5.5	5.5

* Indicates significant difference between the two groups,

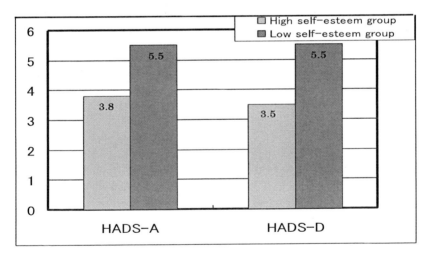

Figure 1. Mean HADS scores in the high- and low- self-esteem groups.
A higher score indicates a higher level of symptoms.
HADS-A: anxiety, HADS-D: depression.

Overall anxiety and depression, as reflected by HADS-A and HADS-D, were not significantly different among treatment modalities and disease stages. Cull et al. [36] showed that 33% of cervical cancer survivors with Stage1b disease, treated by surgery or radiation, were depressed at a mean of 97 weeks after treatment. This was the only study that specifically covered anxiety and depression in cervical cancer survivors [25]. Therefore, the level of anxiety and depression is still not clear for cervical cancer survivors. Moreover, factors that may influence survivors' psychological distress, such as treatment modalities and disease stages, were not clearly described in previous studies. A few studies have shown that levels of clinical depression in gynecologic cancer survivors up to five years post-diagnosis are elevated compared to healthy controls [37]. Bradley et al. [37] studied QOL and mental health in cervical and endometrial cancer survivors and concluded that treatment modality and stage of disease were not related to mood. These findings support the results of the present study, which showed that treatment modalities and disease stages did not make significant differences for anxiety and depression among cervical cancer survivors.

There are limited studies focused on self-esteem in adult cancer survivors. Bertero [38] examined self-esteem and QOL and suggested that lowered self-esteem was recognized in 73.3% of breast cancer patients. Additionally, lowered self-esteem was associated with psychosocial perspectives including negative affections, anger, hostility, absurdity, and low satisfaction with life. Katz et al. [39] examined self-esteem in cancer patients, and concluded that self-esteem was lowered in 20-50% of the patients. Tuinman et al. [27] studied the predictive effects of self-esteem and social support on mental health and concluded that men who are single when they are diagnosed with testicular cancer and remain single are a vulnerable group in relation to self-esteem and mental health. Yap and Davies found that for gynecologic cancer survivors who experienced gonadal failure and infertility, the most common long-term side effects were lowered self-esteem and lowered quality of life [40].

The present paper is the first study to examine the differences of psychological distress depending on the cancer survivors' self-esteem. Anxiety and depression levels in the high self-esteem group were significantly lower than those in the low self-esteem group. Despite facing similar difficulties, survivors with high self-esteem tend to think positively, whereas patients with low self-esteem tend to feel negatively.

The current study had some limitations. We used a convenience sample, which limits the generalizability of the findings to other cervical cancer patients. In addition, this is a cross-sectional study, and a longitudinal study with a larger sample size would be needed to identify the related variables in the course of the treatment. Nevertheless, our results strongly highlighted the importance of self-esteem as an influencing factor of psychological adjustment among cervical cancer survivors.

CONCLUSION

The findings indicated that psychosocial assessment and support are necessary beyond cervical cancer treatment, regardless of type of radiotherapy and disease stages. Addressing these factors may contribute to survivors' self-esteem and be a key factor in preserving and improving patients' psychological state and QOL. Psychosocial intervention with consideration of self-esteem should start as early as possible to alleviate psychosocial distress in cervical cancer survivors.

3. SPIRITUAL NEEDS IN CANCER PATIENTS AND SPIRITUAL CARE BASED ON LOGOTHERAPY [9]

Introduction

In this study, Noguchi et al. [9] suggested the suitability of Frankl's Logotherapy for the spiritual care (psychotherapy) of cancer patients. The aims of the study were to elucidate the complicated structure of spirituality in cancer patients in order to identify possible approaches to spiritual care and the means of evaluating such care among.

It is clear that the experience of having cancer is one of the most shocking life-threatening experiences. As the disease progresses, patients are placed under various types of stress and often present with mental symptoms such as anxiety or depression [41].

Particularly when patients enter the end-of-life stage, they are prone to fear of approaching death and suffer from a sense of solitude and alienation; anxiety and irritation increase. In the field of palliative care, the interest is increasing in the significance of spiritual pain which derives from "loss of meaning". It is reported that about one-half of terminally ill patients describe apparent spiritual pain. There are also those who give non-verbal expression to such pain.

Therefore in order to cope with such severe and radical pain, the patient should be given assistance in finding the meaning of life and personal existence and achieving forgiveness and reconciliation in these areas,; however we need to know more about how spiritual support can be offered towards the aim of discovering the value of life. To address this need, the present paper examined possibilities for delivery of spiritual care (psychotherapy) based on Frankl's existential analytical therapy (logotherapy), as proposed primarily by Breitbert et al. at Memorial Sloan-Kettering Cancer Center in the United States. [42][43]

Methods

In this study, FACIT-Sp (Functional Assessment of Chronic Illness Therapy--Spiritual Well-Being, Japanese version) as already standardized, the PIL (Purpose in Life) test (Japanese version) which was designed according to Frankl's theory, and WHO- Subjective Inventory (WHO-SUBI Japanese version) were used to measure healthfulness and fatigue of spirituality. The participants in this study were patients with cancer selected from the population of inpatients and outpatients at the Research Center Hospital for Charged Particle Therapy, National Institute of Radiological Sciences, Chiba, Japan during the 3-month period from January to March, 2003. Patients were included in the study only if (1) they had been told of their cancer diagnosis; (2) they were 18 years of age or older; (3) the time between their first visit to the hospital and the study was longer than 1 month; (4) their condition was not so severe that they could not complete the questionnaire and participate in a brief interview; and (5) they had no severe mental disorders or dementia. From those who met the inclusion criteria, 320 patients were asked to participate in the study. After providing detailed information on the purpose of the study, informed consent in writing was obtained from 298 patients. Twenty-two patients did not wish to participate in the study because they did not want to talk about their disease. The average age of the patients was 63.0 years, and male patients accounted for 54.4% of the subjects. More than 10 years of education was reported by 80.5% of subjects, and 91.3% were married. Most (58.4%) of the patients were Performance Status (PS) =0, and the majority were in good physical condition. The primary cancer site most frequently reported was the prostate gland (23.8%), and the uterus was the second most common site (23.5%).

Results

The results of the study demonstrated that importance should be placed on two elements – Spirituality and Negative thinking – when we approach the spiritual care of cancer patients. Attention should be given to positive elements (positive thinking) in their attitudes, such as "a forward-looking viewpoint, hope, and meaning in life", as well as the negative elements (negative thinking), which embrace anxiety. Full consideration must be given to the directivity of the two elements and the effects should be fully assessed.

The results also demonstrated the similarities of the concept of spirituality as expressed in the PIL test and FACIT-Sp12. The results also support the use of Frankl's logotherapy for the spiritual care of cancer patients and FACIT-Sp12 appears to be a useful measure of beneficial effects. These results supported the use of "meaning-centered psychotherapy (spiritual care)" as performed by Breitbert et al. of Memorial Sloan-Kettering Cancer Center in the U.S. [42].

Discussion

Frankl stressed the existential character of human beings, who make responsible decisions based on free will and who search for meaning and value in life up to its last moments. He also stressed that ultimate and desperate conditions and suffering in itself do not annihilate the dignity of human beings or the meaning of life. Dignity is annihilated only by the suffering of the patient when "meaning" cannot be found. Thus, Frankl posited the importance of the search for "meaning" [44][45].

Frankl proposed a shifting of viewpoint from "What can we expect of life?" to one of "What does life expect of us?" [46]. He emphasized that meaning can be found up to the last moment of life, no matter how severe the final conditions may be, through recognizing the following three values: (1) the value of creativity (which can be achieved by acting, creating or working); (2) the value of experience (which is found in nature and art and in the love of our fellow human beings); (3) the value of attitudes or character (which depend on our own will, which can rise above extreme, unavoidable and inescapable circumstances) [44][45].

Logotherapy, based on this scheme of thinking, appears to be applicable to the spiritual care of terminally ill patients, if attention is focused on the value of "attitude".

Summary for Three Studies

The two studies by Matsushita et al. [7] and Kobayashi et al. [8] indicated that psychosocial assessment and support is important especially in the pretreatment period to prevent psychological distress of gynecologic cancer patients throughout and beyond the treatment. Generally speaking, anxiety prevention would be especially important in the pretreatment period, and prevention of depression is necessary in the post treatment period.

Psychotherapeutic measures should be designed to reduce stress, enhance coping with stress that cannot be reduced, and establish support systems to maximize adaptation [47]. Logotherapy presented above [8] might be helpful especially for the patients with advanced cancer. Psychotherapy, medical crisis counseling, crisis intervention, family therapy, group therapy, cognitive behavioral therapy, or interpersonal therapy can be used to help the patient to express fears, anxieties, rage, helplessness, and hopelessness related to stressors [48] among women with gynecologic cancer.

REFERENCES

[1]   Jemal, A., Siegel, R., Ward, E., Murray, T., Xu, J., Thun, M.J. (2007).Cancer Statistics 2007. *CA Cancer J Clin,* 57, 43-66.

[2]   Matsusita, T., Murata, H., Matsushima E, Sakata Y, Miyasaka N, Aso T. (2005). Psychological State and Coping Style Among Gynecological Inpatients Undergoing Surgery. *Japanese Journal of General Hospital Psychiatry,* 117(2), 171-179.

[3]   Auchincloss and McCartney, (1998).

[4]   Landoni, F., Maneo, A., Colombo, A. et al. (1997). Randomized study of radical surgery versus radiotherapy for stage Ib-IIa vervical cancer. *Lancet,* 350 (9077), 535-545.

[5]   Ohno, T., Kakinuma, S., Kato, S., Tsujii, H., and Shimada, Y. (2006). Risk of second cancers after radiotherapy for cervical cancer. *Expert Rev. Anticancer Ther,* 6 (1), 49-57.

[6]   Vistad, I., Fossa, S.D., Dahl, A.A. (2006).A critical review of patient-rated quality of life studies of long-term survivors of cervical cancer. *Gynecol Oncol,* 102, 563-572.

[7]   Matsushita, T., Murata, H., Matsushima, E., Sakata, Y., Miyasaka, N., and Aso, T. (2007). Emotinoal state and coping style among

gynecologic patients undergoing surgery. *Psychiatry and Clinical Neurosciences*, 61, 84-93.

[8]   Kobayashi, M., Ohno, T., Matsuda, A., Noguchi, W., Matsushima, E., Kato, S., and Tsuji, H. *Psychological Distress and Quality of life in Cervical Cancer Survivors after Radiotherapy: Do Treatment Modalities, Disease Stage, and Self-esteem Influence Outcomes?* In submission.

[9]   Noguchi, W., Morita, S., Ohno, T., Aihara, O., Tsujii, H., Shimozuma, K., and Matsushima, E. (2006). Spiritual Needs in Cancer Patients and Spiritual Care based on Logotherapy. *Support Care Cancer,* 14 (1), 65-70.

[10] MacNair, D.M., Lorr, M., Droppleman, L.F. (1992). *Profile of Mood States Manual.* Educational and Industrial Testing Service, San Diego.

[11] Akabayashi, A., Yokoyama, K., Araki, S. et al. (1991). *Clinical applications of the Japanese edition of Profile of Mood States (POMS).* Shinshin-Igaku, 31, 577-582 (in Japanese).

[12] Yokoyama, K., Araki, S. (2002). *Japanese POMS Manual.* Kanekoshiten, Tokyo, (in Japanese).

[13] MacCartney, C.F., Larson, D.B. (1987). Quality of life in patients with gynecologic cancer. *Cancer,* 60 (8 Suppl.), 2129-2136.

[14] Cain, E.N., Kohorn, E.I., Quinlan, D.M., Schwartz, P.E., Latimer, K., Rogers, L. (1983). Psychosocail reactions to the diagnosis of gynecologic cancer. *Obstet. Gynecol,* 62, 635-641.

[15] Anderson, B.L., Jochimsen, P.R. (1985). Sexual functioning among breast cancer, gynecologic cancer, and healthy women. *J. Consult. Clin. Psychol,* 53, 25-32.

[16] Auchincloss, S.S. (1995). After treatment. Psychosocial issues in gynecologic cancer survivorship. *Cancer,* 76 (Suppl. 10), 2117-2124.

[17] Maughan, K., Clarke, C. (2001).The effect of a clinical nurse specialist in gynaecological oncology on quality of life and sexuality. *J. Clin. Nurs,* 10, 221-229.

[18] Andersen, B.L. (1985). Sexual functioning morbidity among cancer survivors. Current status and future research directions. *Cancer,* 55, 1835-1842.

[19] Anderson, B., Lutgendorf, S. (1997). Quality of life in gynecologic cancer survivors. *CA Cancer. J. Clin,* 47, 218-225.

[20] Andersen, B.L., Anderson, B., deProsse, C. (1989). Controlled prospective longitudinal study of women with cancer. II. Psychological outcomes. *J. Consult. Clin. Psychol,* 57, 692-697.

[21] Cull, A., Cowie, V.J., Farquharson, D.I., Livingstone, J.R., Smart, G.E., Elton, R.A. (1993). Early stage cervical cancer: Psychosocial and sexual outcomes of treatment. *Br. J.Cancer,* 68, 1216-1220.
[22] Matsushita, T., Matsushima, E., Maruyama, M. (2005). Anxiety and depression of patients with digestive cancer. *Psychiatry Clin. Neurosci,* 59, 576-583
[23] Bodurka-Bevers, D., Basen-Engquist, K., Carmack, C.L. et al. (2000). Depression, anxiety, and quality of life in patients with epithelial ovarian cancer. *Gynecol. Oncol,* 78, 302-308.
[24] Lutgendorf, S.K., Anderson, B., Ullrich, P. et al. (2002). Quality of life and mood in women with gynecologic cancer: A one year prospective study. *Cancer,* 94, 131-140.
[25] Parkin, D.M., Bray, F., Ferlay, J., Pisani, P. (2005). Global cancer statistics, 2002. *CA Cancer J Clin,* 55 (2), 74-108.
[26] Vistad, I., Fossa, S.D., Dahl, A.A. (2006). A critical review of patient-rated quality of life studies of long-term survivors of cervical cancer. *Gynecol Oncol,* 102, 563-572.
[27] Tuinman, M.A., Hoekstra, H.J., Fleer, J., Sleijfer, D., Hoekstra-Weebers, J. (2006). Self-esteem, social support, and mental health in survivors of testicular cancer: a comparison based on relationship status. *Urol Oncol,* 24, 279-286.
[28] Rosenberg, M. (1965). Society and the adolescent self-image. *Princeton* (NJ), USA: Princeton University Press.
[29] Zigmond, A.S., Snaith, R.P. (1983). The hospital anxiety and depression scale. *Acta Psychiat Scand,* 67, 361-370.
[30] Kitamura,T.(1993).Hospital anxiety and depression scale (in Japanese). *Seishinkashindangaku,* 4, 371-372.
[31] Kugaya, A., Akechi, T., Okumura, H. et al. (1998). Screening for psychological distress in Japanese cancer patients. *Jpn J Clin Oncol,* 28, 333-338.
[32] Snaith, R.P. (2003). The hospital anxiety and depression scale. *Health Qual Life Outcomes,* 1, 29-32.
[33] Herrmann, C. (1997). International experiences with the hospital anxiety and depression scale, a review of validation and clinical results. *J Psychosom Res,* 42, 17-41.
[34] Carroll, B.T., Kathol, R.G., Noyes, R.Jr., Wald, T.G., Clamon, G.H. (1993). Screening for depression and anxiety in cancer patients using the hospital anxiety and depression scale. *Gen Hosp Psychiatry,* 15, 69-74.

[35] Yamamoto, M., Matsui, Y., Yamanari, Y. (1982). The structure of perceived aspects of self (in Japanese). *Jpn J of Edu Psychol,* 30, 64-68.

[36] Cull, A., Cowie, V.J., Farquharson, D.I., Livingstone, J.R., Smart, G.E., Elton, R.A. (1993). Early stage cervical cancer: psychosocial and sexual outcomes of treatment. *Br J Cancer,* 68, 1216-1220.

[37] Bradley, S., Rose, S., Lutgendorf, S., Costanzo, E., Anderson, B. (2006). Quality of life and mental health in cervical and endometrial cancer survivors. *Gynecol Oncol,* 100, 479-486.

[38] Bertero, C.M. (2002). Affected self-respect and self-value: The impact of breast cancer treatment on self-esteem and QOL. *Psychooncology,* 11, 356-364.

[39] Katz, M.R., Rodin, G., Devins, G.M. (1995). Self-esteem and cancer: theory and research. *Can J Psychiatry,* 40, 608-615.

[40] Yap, J.K., Davies, M. (2007). Fertility preservation in female cancer survivors. *J Obstet Gynaecol,* 27, 390-400.

[41] Murata, H. (2003). Spiritual pain and its care in patients with terminal cancer: Construction of a conceptual framework by philosophical approach. *Palliative and Supportive Care,* 1, 15-21.

[42] Breitbart, W. (2002). Spirituality and meaning in supportive care: spirituality- and meaning-centered group psychotherapy intervention in advanced cancer. *Support Care Cancer,* 10, 272-280.

[43] McClain, C.S., Rosenfeld, B., Breitbart, W. (2002). Effect of spiritual well-being on end-of-life despair in terminally-ill cancer patients. *Lancet,* 361, 1603-07.

[44] Kearney, M., Mount, B. (2000). Spiritual care of the dying patient. In Chochinov H, Breitbart W eds. *Handbook of Palliative Medicine.* Oxford University Press, New York,USA, 357-73.

[45] Frankl, V.E. (2000). Man's Search for meaning. An Introduction to Logotherapy Houghton Mifflin.

[46] Nagpal, R., Sell, H. (1985). *Subjective Well-being. SEARO Regional Health Papers, 7.* New Delhi: Regional Office for South-East Asia, World Health Organization.

[47] Moadel, A.B., Ostroff, J.S., and Schantz, S.P. (1998). In: *Holland J. Psycho-Oncology.* New York, USA: Oxford University Press, 314-323.

[48] Strain, J. J. (1998). Adjustment Disorder. In: Holland Jeditor. *Psycho-Oncology.* New York, USA: Oxford University Press, 509-517.

INDEX

I